NEW ENGLAND
PIE

HISTORY UNDER A CRUST

ROBERT S. COX

AMERICAN PALATE

DUXBURY FREE LIBRARY

Published by American Palate
A Division of The History Press
Charleston, SC 29403
www.historypress.net

First published 2015

Manufactured in the United States

ISBN 978.1.62619.772.5

Library of Congress Control Number: 2015947047

CONTENTS

INTRODUCTION

The pie is an English institution, which, planted on American soil, forthwith ran rampant and burst forth into an untold variety of genera and species. Not merely the old traditional mince pie, but a thousand strictly American seedlings from that main stock, evinced the power of American housewives to adapt old institutions to new uses. Pumpkin pies, cranberry pies, huckleberry pies, cherry pies, green-currant pies, peach, pear, and plum pies, custard pies, apple pies, Marlborough-pudding pies—pies with top crusts, and pies without— pies adorned with all sorts of fanciful flutings and architectural strips laid across and around, and otherwise varied, attested the boundless fertility of the feminine mind, when once let loose in a given direction.
—Harriet Beecher Stowe, Old Town Folks

M arie Antoinette made quite a splash back in the day when she dismissed a mob of French peasants with the words, "Let them eat cake." As any good Frenchmen would, they responded with pitchforks and revolution and a touch of guillotine, but imagine instead that the queen of New England had said, "Let them eat pie." The response, I suspect, would be different. Here, her good subjects would have less pitch to their forks, and they might call out, "Why thank you, yes, I will have a slice." And that would be all the slicing there was that day. It would be wedges all around.

New England is a pie-loving culture in a pie-loving nation, and the fillings are deep. Anthropologists have observed that food and foodways are among the strongest cultural markers we have. Shared collectively within a culture, even a family, foodways are owned by all who participate in them, and they define who belongs and who does not. We are what we eat in a very real sense, and above all, what we eat (and do not) suggests who we wish to be. Eating traditional, eating healthy, eating local, eating exotic or eating a paleo diet all reveal attitudes toward where we fit in the world, and everything associated with food is part of the picture. Who prepares it and how, how it is served and when and how we write about it are all ways of claiming to belong and ways of distinguishing our culture from others. Learning to cook and eat is to learn where we fit in life, and it is no surprise that long after we surrender such markers as dress or art or even language, our food preferences remain strong.

New England's pies are more than just treats; they are maps for understanding. Pie can be indulgent or frugal, a host for ephemeral fruits or a coffin for the leftovers of the long months of winter. They can be sweet or savory, delicate or robust, healthy or deadly. They are like the New England weather: if you don't like it now, wait a day. As we will see, pies in New England are expressions of the values we place on sociality, thrift, austerity and innovation; they can stand in for the bounty of our soils or our ability to make do with what is on hand.

It hardly seems necessary to define what a pie is, as we all think we know one when we see one, but since this is a book about pie, it is not out of place to try. The problem is that no one seems quite to agree, and from as far back as the fourteenth century, as *The Oxford Companion to Food* points out, the term has steadily evolved, shifting and shading from place to place and generation to generation. At first glance, we can see that the term has little to do with the filling: anything belongs in any combination. Meats, fruits, nuts, dairy, custards, puddings, live birds and even dancing girls are all permissible in certain contexts. Methods of preparation are no better guide. Even the origins of the word give us precious little to go on. According to the *Companion*, pie may be derived from *magpie*, the notoriously larcenous crow. It speculates that the term reflects the magpie's habit of stuffing a hodgepodge of purloined goods in its nest, just like the odd hodgepodges our medieval forebears stuffed. That hardly stands for a definition.

Historian Janet Clarkson did as well as anyone in defining the term, although she came up with a mere two "laws" of pie. First, she wrote, pies must have pastry. "No pastry, no pie." Yet even with this unequivocal statement, she admitted that actual results may vary. Europeans often insist that it takes two crusts to make a true pie, top and bottom, while latitudinarian Americans may slink by with just one. Still, nearly everyone agrees that some

Above: The Mont Blanc of flour: a future crust. *Photo by I. Eliot Wentworth, 2014.*

Right: Butter and flour on the mix. *Photo by I. Eliot Wentworth, 2014.*

pastry crust is a good guide—everyone, that is, except perhaps for fans of the graham cracker.

Second, Clarkson insisted that pies must be baked, not fried, boiled or steamed. Going back far enough in history, she may have a point, as the pie was all about the oven. But we know that our southern cousins are willing to deep fry everything, including pies, and it takes little effort to find examples of pies that are chilled, frozen or, who knows, even sun-dried. Baking alone will not do.

Accepting that laws are made to be broken and moving on, let us abandon all hope of a definition and use the term *pie* pragmatically to refer to anything commonly called a pie, deducing the rest: pies are (usually) baked, they are (usually) baked in some kind of a dish (usually a pie dish) and they (usually) have a crust or crusts.

In some ways, the crust is the key, or at least it is the one thing that most food historians cling to as a defining trait. In early pies, the crust was little more than an enclosure for the ingredients, juices and flavors as the pie baked. Early crusts were a thick and dry-as-dust admixture of flour and water, intended to stand up both to gravity and the heat of the oven. It was, in effect, a medieval baking dish, a container, and not necessarily something to be eaten (though it may have been by the poor). Called "coffins" because of their function, enclosing the body of pie, rather than their effect on the consumer, these crusts had two additional, desirable effects: they were thick enough to exclude air from the filling and thus inhibit spoilage, and they were solid enough to make transport easy. They were, in effect, airtight mailing containers, some as small as a palm and others large enough to fit a pig. As lard (a rich man's ingredient) and butter (for the poor) became more common in the eighteenth century, crusts edged toward the edible, the flaky and crumbly, and when Crisco vegetable shortening was introduced in 1911 (and its arch-rival, Spry, in 1936), home cooks had a range of options, some of which were even pure. Crusts henceforth had the opportunity to shine on their own.

Although fewer New Englanders than ever claim English roots, our pie culture is certainly English in origin, though shaped by centuries of ethnic, racial, political, agricultural and social change. In that time, our nation has become urbanized, industrialized, diversified, electrified and atomized, and the roles of women and men, white and black, immigrant and native, have shifted so dramatically that one can hardly imagine a food that could remain constant.

Yet pie has remained our constant companion, even as pies evolve. From Puritan theology to the revolutionary ideology, American pies have been shaped by an increasing preference for culinary simplicity. Even early in the colonial era, Americans began to distinguish themselves from their English cousins in cooking, partly by the drift that naturally results from distance and autonomy, partly by the circumstances of living in a new world and climate and partly from religious predilections for simplicity associated especially with the Puritans. While upper-class English cooks were emulating the French in their reverence for ornate dishes, elaborate sauces, dainty ingredients and sharp social distinctions, most Americans turned toward simpler fare that harmonized with the spiritual values of restraint and discipline. Colonists who traveled in English circles, literally or by correspondence, may have labored hard to shed the stigma of "colonial" rubehood, and many of our elite may still have aspired to metropolitan sophistication. Yet in the practical matters of day-to-day life, American preferences were middling, plain and content.

The trend toward divergence from England picked up steam after the American Revolution, when the desire to perfect our independence took hold. Hard won as it was, political independence was necessary, but not sufficient, for the most ardent Patriots—we required a new revolution to create a cultural independence in literature, the arts and sciences and, of course, cuisine. Historian James McWilliams wrote that Americans began to fashion a cuisine reflecting the values associated with the new republican form of government—values that in some small ways echoed Puritan values. Rejecting anything that smacked of aristocracy or European decadence, American cooks were drawn to the austere and direct in cooking and began to embrace American ingredients. According to McWilliams, we "embraced the rough edges of American foodways to foster a pastoral ideal that promoted the frontier values that the colonists had once downplayed."

Rustic, plebeian and plain, the pie fit. Americans seized on their rustic reputation and made it a virtue, lauding the superiority of simple fare and bumptious manners. British travelers in the 1830s, like the imperious Frances Trollope, were aghast:

> *I will not draw any comparisons between a good dinner party in the two countries. It is rarely they dine in society, except in taverns and boarding houses. Then they eat with the greatest possible rapidity, and in total silence; I have heard it said by American ladies, that the hours of greatest enjoyment to the gentlemen were those in which a glass of gin cocktail, or egging, receives its highest relish from the absence of all restraint whatever; and when there were no ladies to trouble them.*

The ordinary mode of living is abundant, but not delicate. They consume an extraordinary quantity of bacon. Ham and beaf-steaks appear morning, noon, and night. In eating, they mix things together with the strangest incongruity imaginable. I have seen eggs and oysters eaten together: the sempiternal ham with apple-sauce; beefsteak with stewed peaches; and salt fish with onions…There is a great want of skill in the composition of sauces; not only with fish, but with every thing.

In Trollope's eyes, Americans were unrepentantly crude, low-class and content. They were an affront to any status-conscious traveler. Trollope was particularly struck by the American passion for dessert, "invariably pronounced desart," which only confirmed their low status. "They are 'extravagantly fond,' to use their own phrase," she wrote, "of puddings, pies, and all kinds of 'sweets,' particularly the ladies." Americans wallowed in the ignoble—even women, who by virtue of gender were theoretically our best hope for refinement.

Of course, it was not quite so simple. Few working people had the luxury of rejecting anything, aristocracy or otherwise. They got by. It is all too easy to speak of a New England penchant for frugality when pointing to persuasively brilliant writers like Lydia Maria Child, but when she preached about the values of frugality and republicanism, she preached a frugality of the elite imposed on the poor, who lived frugality by necessity. It is all too easy to slip into generalities and speak of our pies as "English" or plain or native, when they actually represent a complex history of adaptation to ingredients and culture that forms and reforms generation by generation. The tumult of the Industrial Revolution, the tidal wave of immigration and the disruptions of modern technologies, prepared and processed foods and ideas of the social order had even stronger influence on the direction our pies would take. Given the different classes of New Englanders, with different origins, tastes and ideals, it would be hard to talk about a "New England preference" without specifying which New England we had in mind.

In the following chapters, I will follow these themes through a dozen (or more) of New England's signature pies, one selected for each month of the year. There are other deserving pies, as beloved as these, but the dozen chosen are embedded in the ebb and flow of the seasons, the arrival and departure of ingredients and the comings and goings of people and ideas. "I like pie—and am not ashamed," Anne Warner once wrote. "It is part of a Yankee inheritance, so I even own up to the appetite with modest pride."

JANUARY

French Meat Pie

Somewhere along the way, I convinced Suzette to make a French meat pie for us, a legendary dish in her family reserved only for the short days of the long holiday season. This was not something taken lightly. To be initiated into the mysteries of preparation required trust, and her daughter, Danielle, and I sat quietly by as ingredients were staged on the counter: ground pork and beef set next to onion and mashed potato; cinnamon, cloves and herbs were laid out near a chilled crust. On the surface, it may seem that French meat pie is just another ripple in an endless wave of meat pies, but it is not so. This was a magic pie, and there is nothing in the meat pie world quite like the savory assertiveness of its spuds and spice.

The pie appears only when the family can be gathered around the kitchen—like Danielle, Suzette and I that afternoon—and it is talked into existence more than it is baked. Several family members are convinced of its magical potency. While driving to Virginia one winter, Suzette's other daughter, Michelle, got stranded in a snowstorm with her husband, and just as they began to fear that they would starve and be ravaged by wolves, they discovered that Suzette had nestled a half-pie in the back seat along with a bottle of red wine. If not exactly manna or loaves and fishes, they discovered that with wine enough and time, the miracle of French meat pie could save them.

The recipe that Suzette used that afternoon was an old one, a legacy from her grandmother, and although she admitted to making adjustments over the years to suit the tastes of her too-picky daughters, Suzette swore that on this occasion she would make it just like *mémé* a half century ago, authentic and original. This was the real thing. So, we sat around the kitchen, Danielle and I, watching Suzette work and listening as she apologized repeatedly for failing *meme*: "Grandmother never would never use store-bought"…"I think she used more beef than I do"…"Don't tell anyone about the Bell's."

Of course, I would never tell about the Bell's (quite yet), but after an afternoon of prattling, sautéing, boiling, baking and cooling, we were presented with a brown-hued mound of savory stuff. Made true like this, each slice stood proud, its sides clean and straight, bound silky tight by the invisible bonds of potato. Each slice held its form as it was eaten. It is French Canadian comfort food—rich without being heavy, firm without being dense and with just enough spice to linger on the palate and imprint on the brain.

The mythic roots of French meat pie—and *myth* is the operative word—are thought to extend though Quebec to France and, from there, back to the Middle Ages, even though the potato, that crucial ingredient, was then unknown in Europe. Wherever the pie appeared, its spices and meats made it a distinguished but costly dish, reserved only for special occasions. Whatever the historical particulars, this spiced pork pie, or *tourtière* in French, so instilled itself in French Canada as to be considered a "traditional" entrée

Starting the meat and onions. *Photo by I. Eliot Wentworth, 2015.*

Filling the crust, the potato now rendered to a sheen. *Photo by I. Eliot Wentworth, 2015.*

The French meat pie. *Photo by I. Eliot Wentworth, 2015.*

A slice purloined. *Photo by I. Eliot Wentworth, 2015.*

for the *Réveillon*, the meal served after the Christmas midnight mass. It is central to one of the central religious festivities of the year.

Just as important, after being transported to New England, the French meat pie blossomed as a symbol of French Canadian identity, a culinary mark of cultural membership that has survived language loss and assimilation to become a supermarket staple in neighborhoods where the "French" settled; it is also a blue plate addition to the menus of restaurants like the fabulous Burgundy Brook Café, a mainstay of the food scene in Palmer, Massachusetts, where the owner, Keith Gordon, serves it for breakfast. The recipe, he said, is from his *mémé*'s mother and may be 150 years old.

The word *neighborhood* has a quaint air about it, but in practice, New England has not always been so quaint for immigrants. While zealously building their City on a Hill during the early years of colonization, the authorities in Massachusetts Bay and Plymouth earned a reputation for zeal in expelling nonconformists, transporting them with little delay to the hinterlands of Rhode Island or the wastelands of the West Indies. When not shipping or whipping their Quakers, they executed them.

Among all the nonconformists, Catholics—and especially French Catholics—were lavished with the most attention, thanks to two centuries of imperial rivalry between Britain and France. In our New World "wilderness," only the native inhabitants were more feared than the French as dangers to English order, and with their Jesuit priests, the French represented a theological peril as well. Their colonial stronghold to the north was a burr under the English saddle, and English settlers in Massachusetts Bay responded as they knew best: legally, enacting an anti-priest law in 1647 that imposed death on Jesuits landing on their shores, and in the year of the witch panic at Salem, 1692, they rejected political benefits for Catholics even while extending "toleration" to others. Even tolerant Rhode Island imposed restrictions on the papist horde until the time of the American Revolution, when the rhetoric of universal rights (and the need for French support) temporarily overwhelmed the old hatreds.

The long and bitter imperial struggle between France and England for North American domination, and the even longer religious struggle, left a scar of fear and disdain in the American people. Harvard College could be relied on to sustain the legacy, hosting an annual lecture lambasting "popery," and other educators ensured that even the smallest child would learn the New England way to hate. The famous *New England Primer*—the slender book that taught generations how to read and how to recite the prayer "Now I Lay Me Down to Sleep"—included catchy couplets warning about Catholics:

> *Abhor that arrant whore of Rome,*
> *And all her blasphemies,*
> *And drink not of her cursed cup,*
> *Obey not her decrees.*

Conditions improved gradually after the Revolution, and the Catholic population grew large enough that the Catholic Church officially appointed a bishop of Boston in 1808; still, popular hatred for Catholics roiled on. Religious violence flared up with disturbing regularity, breaking out most spectacularly in August 1834, when Protestant mobs besieged and set flame to the Ursuline convent in Charlestown, Massachusetts. As formal proscriptions faded, Catholics came under political attack, too, by the anti-immigrant Know-Nothing Party, which swept the Massachusetts state elections in 1854.

And yet Catholics continued to arrive on New England shores. The Irish were the first to make a beachhead, driven by generations of crises at home. The debacle of Wolfe Tone's rebellion led to an exodus in the late 1790s, and an outright deluge followed fifty years later in response to the Great Famine.

French Canadians swelled in, too, beginning at midcentury, when Quebec was mired in bleakness and declining productivity and New England was emerging as an industrializing, labor-consuming mecca. Seasonal, unsafe, poorly paid and sporadic though it was, work could be found in the great belching mills and factories, making shoes and textiles, cutlery and precision tools, buttons, boxes, snaths and scythes or any variety of other goods. For the semi-skilled, the unskilled and even small children, the opportunity was there to rise to the lowest rungs of the economic ladder. Leaving their hardscrabble northern lives behind, French immigrants poured into Manchester and Biddeford, Lewiston, Lynn, Lowell, Fall River, Providence and dozens of other towns. In a mere forty years from 1860 to 1900, the French population of New England increased sixteenfold to make up nearly one-tenth of the region's total.

Like many new immigrants, the French often settled in their own discrete enclaves, as historian Ronald A. Petrin noted, living among (but not necessarily with) their English-speaking neighbors. For decades, they resisted assimilation and, in Petrin's words, waged "a determined and well-organized effort to preserve their group identity, a struggle they termed *la Survivance*." Through building their own benevolent societies, their own social clubs, their own candidates for office, their own language and their own churches and schools, their attention to *Survivance* ultimately made a dent in New England culture, culinary and otherwise, shaping their neighbors just as their neighbors shaped them. Versions of the *Survivance* saga played out, too, among the Finnish immigrants, Portuguese, Azoreans and Cape Verdeans, Irish, Italians, Poles, Russians and Lithuanians, transforming modern New England cuisine into a patchwork of English roots and immigrant tastes, all adapted to our frigid climate and flinty soil.

Suzette was a second-generation Franco-American, a product of the tail end of the great migration. Born in the Northern Kingdom of Vermont and raised in a French-speaking home in a largely French neighborhood far up in Caribou, Maine, she lived her French identity as she learned to be a Yankee. Her birth name, Gravel, was originally pronounced in the Americanized way, as if she were a small chip of stone, but her mother, Nora (née Bossé) agreed to marry into the family only if the name was given a French twist: "Gra-*vell*." Ever since, there have been Gravels and Gravels, cousins separated by a gulf of pronunciation.

Just as Gravel became Gravel, so too did *tourtière* become French meat pie, an Americanized version that remembers its French Canadian roots as it evolves. Wherever French speakers roamed in Canada, the *tourtière* traveled with. In the 1880s, according to travel writer Charles Elliott, it even traveled coast to coast as a headlining entrée aboard the Canadian Pacific Transcontinental Railway. Everywhere it went, *tourtière* transmogrified itself to suit regional tastes and the local availability of foods, not to mention the whims of individual cooks. At some level, it hardly changed: ground meat and potatoes remained its body and onions, spices and herbs its soul. Beyond this framework, though, chaos reigned. While some cooks called only for pork, others added beef or were converted to veal, poultry, hare or wild game. Vegetables are not entirely a foreign concept, with root vegetables like carrots considered blessings by some and sins by others, and celery and garlic offered—or required—atonement. Surprisingly, even potatoes could be considered optional. While cooing over the many varieties of French meat pie, the author of *Le Festival Franco-Americain*, a cookbook from South Hadley, Massachusetts, said on the side, "We are told that the pie included potatoes only if the family was not very rich and had to make the meat go further." The Gravels always used potatoes, Danielle told me proudly, "just like peasants."

The herbs, spices and add-ins were the means by which cooks truly distinguished themselves. This was, after all, a spiced meat pie. In various doses and combinations, the quartet of allspice, cinnamon, cloves and nutmeg formed the background of every mouthful of *tourtière*, but there is more here than meets the pie. Cloves and cinnamon are nearly de rigeur in *tourtières* (the Canadian version), almost always appearing together and often, but not always, with the companionship of nutmeg and allspice. But after crossing the border to become French meat pie, the *tourtière* lost much of its spicy soul. Many French meat pies omit spices altogether, and in those where they are retained, the most common spice is not clove but allspice, which can even appear alone.

Herbs and add-ins are another field for cooks to display their prowess. A drenching of apple cider, cognac or wine (white or red) enlivens a pie; eggs add texture; and garlic, ginger, celery seed or mushrooms play well with the basic mix. Herbs are not uncontroversial. Perhaps half the recipes for French meat pie include an herb component, usually dried and ground. Sage, thyme and bay, in that order, abound, with savory, rosemary and *herbes de Provence* entertaining the adventurous.

And thus we come to Suzette's shame: Bell's Poultry seasoning. Over the years, Suzette had subtly adjusted her *mémé*'s recipe to suit her family's tastes and, frankly, to make preparation more convenient. She never went so far as the blessed cook who relied on dried onion soup mix, but Suzette knew how to silence her too-picky daughters: dispense with the clove and sage she once loved in favor of the convenience of a commercial spice mix, Bell's Poultry Seasoning. Like many before and since, Suzette turned to a local substitute. First sold in 1867, Bell's is a favorite quirk for flavoring turkey in New England, and its addictive mix of rosemary, oregano, sage, ginger, marjoram and thyme is not so far afield from other French meat mixes as to be unrecognizable. As substitutes go, it was fine, but for Suzette, it was apostasy on the order of using store-bought crust (which she also did).

The topic of Bell's might not have been sensitive had Suzette's five-year-old granddaughter Sophie not ended a meal recently with the emphatic declaration, "Maybe you should lay off the Bell's, Grandma." Too much of a good thing, after all. Suzette's sensitivity on the matter was further inflamed when I suggested that some of the leftover gravy from the accompanying turkey would be a nice addition. No one in the family had considered it before, but soon enough, they all warmed to the gravy, reciting the phrase "let's cover up the Bell's." More change from tradition was added to more change.

To be clear, Suzette was horrified that I would even think to mention Bell's, but she consoled herself with the knowledge that if I wrote about it, as she put it, "Well, at least no one will read it." But for all her concern over deviating from the true French path and turning away from *mémé*, Suzette simply did what nearly every French meat pie cook had done before: adapt creatively to the changing conditions and tastes and surrender to the sirens of availability and convenience. Her Bell's pie is different, but not more different than dozens of other recipes, and the twists and turns she introduced have ultimately created a taste in her family for the good Yankee Bell's—at least until the younger generation broke ranks (they have grown to love its subtler assets). Her choice of ingredients reflects the true history of a border-crossing, language-defying pie, and it has become a pie the family loves, a pie that brings them together each year to talk once again into being.

So it has been with New Englanders. The struggle to be true to our past and true to the present is always a negotiation within. When Suzette moved to Easthampton, Massachusetts, as a young mother, she found a community with three distinct Catholic parishes: Notre Dame du Bon Conseil for the French, Sacred Heart of Jesus for the Poles and Immaculate Conception for the Irish. Even as the industrial base of this quintessential mill town frayed and the mills began to close, each of the churches clung to its parishioners, each with its language, its masses, its schools, its schedules and, most of all, its food. But by 2010, the diocese had determined that it had reached a point where separate churches could no longer be sustained, and the three were merged into the sunny Our Lady of the Valley. Adapting, creatively, the three groups of parishioners have worked to create a new family union while holding fast to their distinct identities. Polish masses are still held once a month, the Knights of Columbus holds an annual French Night dinner and every June, Polish pierogi and golumpki are served at the Parish Festival for Our Lady of the Valley right next to sharp-edged slices of French meat pie. *Survivance* in a crust.

RECIPES

Nora's French Meat Pie (With Suzette's Additions)

2 lbs. ground beef (80/20)
1 lb. ground pork
1 potato, boiled and mashed
¼ tsp. black pepper
¼–½ tsp. each sage, cloves, cinnamon, to taste
¼ tsp. thyme
pinch of nutmeg
1 small onion, minced fine
double pie crust (store-bought works fine)
4 pats butter

Combine meats, onion, and seasoning well and simmer, covered, for 30 minutes, stirring the meat to break it up several times. Drain off liquid. Let stand for fat to rise to top and discard fat; return the rest of the liquid to the meat. Combine with mashed potato. Place in pastry-lined pie tin. Cover with top crust and place 4 pats of butter evenly on top. Bake at 400 degrees for 25 minutes or until browned. Meat mixture may be made the day before and refrigerated until ready to use. Makes one 9-inch pie. Great for brunch buffet.

SUZETTE'S VARIATIONS:
- Alter the ratio of beef to pork to 50:50.
- Double the amount of potato.

- Omit the thyme, cinnamon and, usually, the onion.
- Substitute Bell's Poultry Seasoning with (optionally) a pinch of ground sage and ground cloves.

French Meat Pie (Turquaire) (Volunteer Women, 1950)

3 lbs. Ground pork sausage
1 large onion, chopped
8 or 9 medium potatoes, ground
1 teaspoon salt, scant
1 teaspoon sage
1 teaspoon cinnamon
½ teaspoon cloves
2½ cups water

Simmer onion under pork for 10 minutes, add remainder of ingredients and simmer for ½ hour. This is enough filling for three pies. Use a standard pie crust recipe. Avoid too "short" a crust due to the rich filling. Pie may be stored in deep freeze and reheated. Serve with catsup or chili sauce.—Mrs. M.L. Decker.

FEBRUARY

The Rich Burgomaster of the Provisions

It is February in New England, and everywhere is frost-white and frozen, except perhaps the dead ends of the "Deep South" like Bridgeport or New Haven. There are times, entire weeks really, when daylight falls, the temperature dives and all becomes snow-wrapped and silent. The world seems to end at the front door. On days like this, all a person wants is a blanket, a fire and the consolation that comes from the comfort of pie. It is tradition. It is New England. Who among us cannot hear the still sound of a knife burgling into a fresh crust or imagine a plume of steam rising, ghostly, above? Who cannot warm to the memory of the fork and brighten just a bit?

Of all the pies in a New England winter, few are more welcome than the round savory flavors of poultry. Long before there was a New England, poultry pies flourished in the multitude. The English luxuriated in them, wolfing them down year round but seeking them specially whenever the weather turned foul. Eighteenth-century writers used the term *poultry* loosely, going far beyond the familiar rounds of domesticated chickens, turkeys, geese and ducks. Almost any bird, small or large, could be stuffed into a maw of crust and consumed. If it could fly, it made pie. The extraordinary Charles Carter could not kill birds fast enough to fill up his cookbook in 1732, recording recipes for pies of partridge, goose, quail, sparrow and lark—songbirds beware!—not to mention the ruffs and reifs, curlews and wheat-ears he "potted" and the orrelans and plovers he dispatched. Most of Carter's poultry pies were elaborate affairs, including forcemeat (a mixture of finely ground meat and fat), hard-boiled eggs and a dousing of gravy, but

Rooster, Wendell, Massachusetts. *Photo by Roy Finestone, 1980. Roy Finestone Collection, Special Collections, UMass Amherst Libraries.*

this high-toned chef for the Duke of Argyll went further out on the fancy scale, imitating the best cooks of France by refining his dishes with dainties like asparagus tips, coxcombs and sweetbreads.

If there was a single pie that truly stood out among Carter's multitude, if only because it became so popular, it was pigeon pie. As ghastly as it sounds to dine on a park-dwelling avian rodent, the pigeon pie was part of the century's poultry pantheon and was popular enough to cross the Atlantic and roost in the new United States, where millions of pigeons cooed in our woods or were cooped on our roofs, awaiting slaughter. Topped with a flaky puff pastry, a pigeon pie was typically made of eviscerated birds, whole or split in half, browned and arrayed with "necks, gizzards, livers, pinions, and hearts" (in the artful words of Hannah Glasse) strewn among the corpses, "with a beef steak in the middle." It was as if a pigeon exploded on a cow. Both Carter and Glasse found that this scene could be gussied up *à la française*, which for Glasse meant filling the birds with "a very high force-meat" and adding asparagus tips, artichoke hearts, "mushrooms, truffles, and morels," although she added that the precise mix should be "according to different palates."

In pursuit of further elegance, a cook could also turn attention to presentation. Maria Rundell, for example, crowned her crust with "three feet nicely cleaned, to show what pie it is." Picky when it came to appendages, Rundell warned the prudent cook to select only "supple" feet, since "if old," they would be "harsh." Precisely why she specified three feet remains a mystery to this day, but there is little doubt that a hobbled, odd-numbered bird would ever escape her kitchen.

Pigeons and larks, however, were not the future of New England poultry pie, and the fancier versions from Carter and Glasse were replaced by simpler, more direct preparations. Whole flocks of birds, numerous and diverse, would continue to be encased in pastry, but it was the turkey and (especially) chicken that consumed Americans.

Like other poultry, chickens and turkeys enjoyed a distinguished place in pie stretching much farther back than the earliest years of New England colonization. When Puritans first flooded our shores, chicken pies in England still reflected the ancient love for mixes of sweets, meats and spices in riotous excess. Early cookbooks like the *Compleat Cook* (1658) threw entire chickens under the hard, inedible crust, along with sheep's tongue, veal, mutton, "Chick-heads, Lark, or any such like, Pullets, Coxcombs, Oysters, Calves-Udder" and marrow to make the savory point. To balance this collision of flesh, the cook included marjoram and mace, gooseberries

"Yesterday I was an egg, today I am a chicken, tomorrow I'll be a pie. Ain't life hell?" Gag postcard, circa 1920.

and dates, artichoke hearts, citrus fruits and a bit of white wine and claret. One hundred years later, Glasse still celebrated such excess, incorporating anchovy, citrus, sweetbreads, artichoke hearts, truffles, morels and coxcombs in her chicken pie. Hers was no humble dish, although such exuberance would slowly be tamed.

Across the Atlantic, chicken and turkey pies emerged after the American Revolution as integral parts of our regional cuisine and surprisingly significant contributions to the new sense of our New England selves. As they had done before, and would do again, post-Revolutionary New Englanders began to reimagine their Puritan roots in light of political independence, stitching together a regional identity that, among other things, revolved around the values they associated with their new republican form of government: austerity, moderation, thrift and "liberty." Commingled in the popular imagination with the most New England of holidays, Thanksgiving, chicken and turkey pies became part of the process of nation building.

Although the holiday myth is better told elsewhere, it is enough here to single out the person more responsible than any other for elevating Thanksgiving to national status: Sarah Josepha Hale. A New Hampshire writer and editor of the woman's magazine *Godey's Ladies Book*, Hale waged a decades-long crusade for official recognition of the holiday, with the decisive moment coming during the time of crisis called the Civil War. In 1863,

Hale implored President Lincoln to designate "a National and fixed Union Festival" in the month of November, a time that New Englanders had long venerated. Lincoln concurred. With the desperate wartime desire for national unity and the appeal to a common past too much to resist, Thanksgiving went national, as did the menu associated with it.

Hale's first novel, *Northwood, a New England Tale* (1827), was part of the process of reimagining New England in a post-Revolutionary world and simultaneously a celebration of the middle-class values that she wished to enshrine and an assault on the brutality of southern slavery, which she loathed. Fittingly, at the center of her story was a Thanksgiving celebration at which a roast turkey took pride of place, of course, although here the bird was not alone; chicken pie was its inevitable compatriot:

> *At the foot of the board a sirloin of beef, flanked on either side by a leg of pork and loin of mutton, seemed placed as a bastion to defend innumerable bowls of gravy and plates of vegetables disposed in that quarter. A goose and pair of ducklings occupied side stations on the table, the middle being graced, as it always is on such occasions, by that rich burgomaster of the provisions, called a chicken pie. This pie, which is wholly formed of the choicest parts of fowls, enriched and seasoned with a profusion of butter and pepper, and covered with an excellent puff paste, is, like celebrated pumpkin pie, an indispensable part of a good and true Yankee Thanksgiving; the size of the pie usually denoting the gratitude of the party who prepares the feast.*

The celebration and abundance was testimony to the feelings of the people for one another, of the divine favor showered on the free north and the bounty that our free land produced.

Neither was Hale alone in her love for the "rich burgomaster." Shorn of the fancy ingredients recommended by earlier writers and redirected from its French tendencies, chicken pie became a simpler, though still gravy-rich, center of attention aligned with the new New England. New England writers of all stripes insisted that chicken pie was essential to a proper Thanksgiving meal. For natives of Massachusetts like Esther Howland, the menu could be nothing without chicken pie to wash down the "roast turkey, stuffed," while her fellow Bay Stater Edward Everett Hale (no relation to Sarah) recalled that the holiday commenced "with your chicken pie and your roast turkey...there was no other day on which we had four kinds of pies on the table and plum pudding beside, not to say chicken pie." In the Connecticut novel *Old*

Town Folks, Harriet Beecher Stowe wrote that it took an entire week of concerted family effort to prepare the meal:

> *But who shall do justice to the dinner? Thanksgiving was only the beginning of chicken time. Whatever time of year, chickens presented advantages for those who would eat them: they were cheap, easy to keep, and the hens laid eggs to eat. But in winter, their true advantage shone: timing. Cattle and pigs were usually slaughtered when cold weather set in and the meat was then pickled or salted for long-term storage, but chickens clucked to a different rhythm. Since their flesh not as easily preserved as pork, chickens were usually eaten as soon as they were killed, and although the winter season was not a particularly thriving time for fowl* [at least before the 1922 discovery that they needed sunlight to synthesize vitamin D], *when they were eaten, at least they would be fresh. In winter's doldrums, chicken pies became a respite from the numbing similitude of preserved meats, baked beans, and brown bread suppers. The fresh cheer that chicken pies brought to the winter dark and their rekindling of holiday celebrations cemented their place in our regional cuisine.*

So it was that a few quick generations after Hale and Stowe helped to create a New England past, women like Nellie Brown could be found making a living on New England nostalgia through nostalgic chicken pies. In 1933, Brown turned her family's summer home in Southbury, Connecticut, into the Old Hundred Inn and restaurant, a place that trafficked in "old-time New England food." Everything about the place fit the image, from the cozy dining room with "antique family chairs and tables, Oriental rugs and huge log-burning fireplaces" to the waitresses "dressed in the long, full skirts and tight bodices of a hundred years ago." This was literally a home dressed up as New England history.

By 1939, the star on the Old Hundred menu was chicken pie, served every Saturday night "like mother used to make." A modern version of the venerable dish, it was stripped-down Americana containing chicken boiled with salt pork, deboned and shredded coarse. Drenched in butter (as it should be), the chicken was bathed in broth to make a succulent gravy, but Brown's innovation came in a crust made of light biscuit dough, where the top was rolled out and baked in a separate pan. After it emerged from the oven "crisp and perfect," the toupee was fitted on top and service ensued.

Even as the Old Hundred Inn was peddling nostalgia for the past in its dining room, the future came knocking at the back door. After the Second

World War, Nellie Green formed a partnership with Roy Fulton and Samuel Green to manufacture Old Hundred Ice Cream; the company was eventually purchased by the national brand Baskin Robbins before shuttering its doors when the globalized economy attacked in 1998. But for the generation born when Old Hundred was at its peak, the New England way of eating that it represented was already becoming passé. The roadside inn with its homey decor and memories of yore was giving way to modern dining.

For many baby boomers, the scratch of an aluminum tray on a portable tea table triggers a chain reaction: fork, sit, salivate. It was not just ice cream that was freezing in Connecticut; it was TV dinners. For many, it was frozen chicken pie in particular that set the glands flowing while the television was glowing.

Barely older than the baby boomers themselves, frozen foods are a native industry to New England and can truly be called a regional fixation. Our winters aside, freezing was long recognized as an aid to food preservation, and in the days before electricity and refrigeration, finding a way to achieve it was a fortune waiting to happen, with our vastly profitable fisheries providing the jackpot at the frozen end of the rainbow. When applying for a patent for freezing fish fast in 1861, Enoch Piper of Camden, Maine, saw the problem clearly: "artificial congelation," or putting fish in barrels under crushed ice, was just too slow to freeze fish properly, and the ice was too quick to melt. Furthermore, the fish that escaped rot were often ruined by the large ice crystals that permeated their flesh and destroyed their texture. Piper was not the first to take a whack at commercial freezing, but he did lead to the first commercially frozen fish, and just as important, he inspired other inventors on their way.

When laurels for the frozen foods industry are bestowed, they are usually placed on the ample head of Clarence Birdseye. Dropping out of Amherst College in 1912, Birdseye did what most Lord Jeffs would do under circumstances: go to Labrador to seek a fortune in furs. A literal translation of the name Labrador is "colder than New England," and in that frigid place, Birdseye witnessed the indigenous Inuits take advantage of the climate to freeze their dinners quickly. Flash freezing, he saw, resulted in the formation of minute ice crystals that produced little disruption of the tissue. Whether fish, cabbage, caribou or goose, the foods emerged tasty, unspoiled and texturally intact.

At once, Birdseye's life was changed. When he returned to New York in 1922, he founded Birdseye Seafood Inc. with the goal of developing a quick-freezing machine, and while failure and perseverance are part of the story, by 1924 he had honed in on a process that became a workhorse. His new company, General Seafood Corporation, froze foods between a pair of flat, refrigerated surfaces, and from there, the frozen foods industry took off. Birdseye and his competitors spent enormous energy improving machines during the 1920s and 1930s, and by the end of the Second World War, frozen foods had became a national reality, just in time for the return of the GIs and the suburban revolution.

Patents for commercially producing frozen pies go back to at least the 1930s, when Birdseye's machines were whirring at high pitch. For patentee Martha Thal in 1939, the goal of freezing pie, like the goal at the Old Hundred, was to create a reasonable facsimile of homemade food that could evoke the values of hearth, home and womanhood but would be suited to the modern era. Referencing the traditional family and already feeling the impact of modern technologies and time-saving inventions, she wrote that the "main object" of her invention

> is to commercially produce fruit or other pies for the housewife to bake in her own kitchen at any time, whether in or out of season, that will have the character of a freshly made home made pie…It is a further object of the invention to produce commercially unbaked or raw pies, which may be baked by the housewife without inconvenience and with very little effort.

From Thal to TV, the step was small, and TV dinners spread as quickly as television itself, the new technologies of frozen foods and entertainment developing hand in hand. Frozen dinners first appeared during the war, when Maxson Food Systems began marketing frozen meals to airlines and the military, and by the late 1940s, Jack Fisher's FrigiDinners were being sold to bars and restaurants, though to little success. Retail merchandizing to consumers followed in 1949, when Albert and Meyer Bernstein's Frozen Dinners Inc. began to package dinners in aluminum trays with separate compartments in the Pittsburgh area and selling them under the One-Eyed Eskimo label. Perhaps most famously, in 1953 C.A. Swanson and Sons (which had already introduced frozen chicken pot pies) introduced the name "TV Dinner," trademarking the name by which all others would be known. Although not New Englanders, their motivation in entering the infant frozen foods game is said to have been their search for something to do with Thanksgiving leftovers, and the first TV Dinner was allegedly the Thanksgiving meal of turkey, cornbread stuffing, peas and sweet potatoes.

Familiar and comforting on cold nights, the chicken pie has long represented the values of those who make it. Fancied and refined when served in aristocratic courts, the dish was transformed into a centerpiece of a republican virtue, took pride of place at New England holiday celebrations and then became a memory of the same. Where, then, is the comfort in the single portion, frozen?

RECIPES

Pigeon Pie (Rundell, 1807)

Rub the pigeons with pepper and salt, inside and out; in the latter put a bit of butter, and, if approved, some parsley chopped with the livers, and a litter of the same seasoning. Lay a beef steak at the bottom of the dish, and the birds on it; between every two, a hard egg. Put a cup of water in the dish; and if you have any ham in the house, lay a bit on each pigeon: it is a great improvement to the flavour.

Observe, when ham is cut for gravy or pies, to take the under part rather than the prime.

Season the gizzards, and two joints of the wings, and put them in the centre of the pie; and over them, in a hole made in the crust, three feet nicely cleaned, to show what pie it is.

Chicken Pie (Howland, 1845)

Cut up your chicken, parboil it, season it in the pot, take up the meat, put in a flour thickening, and scald the gravy; make the crust of sour milk made sweet with saleratus, put in a piece of butter or lard the size of an egg; cream is preferable to sour milk, if you have it. Take a large tin pan, line it with the crust, put in your meat, and pour in the gravy from the pot; make it nearly full, cover it over with crust, and leave a vent; bake it in a moderate oven two hours, or two and a half.

Chicken Pie for Thanksgiving
(Lincoln, 1883, Attributed to Miss A. M. Towne)

Two chickens, three pints of cream, one pound of butter, flour enough to make a stiff crust. Cut the chicken at the joints, and cook in boiling salted water till tender.

Crust.—Three pints of cream, one heaping teaspoonful of salt, and flour to mix it hard enough to roll out easily. Line a deep earthen dish having flaring sides with a thin layer of paste. Roll the remainder of the paste half an inch thick. Cut *three quarters of a pound of butter* into small pieces, and put them on the dough quite close together. Sprinkle a little flour over the butter, and roll the paste over and over. Roll out again half an inch thick and roll up. Cut off from the ends of the roll, turn the pieces over and roll out half an inch thick for rims. Wet the paste in the dish with milk, and lay the rims round the sides of the dish. Put on two, three, or four rims, showing one above another, the inside rim the highest. Wet each rim to make it adhere. Fill the centre with the parboiled chicken. Take out some of the larger bones. Season the chicken liquor with *salt* and *pepper*, and pour it over the chicken; use enough to nearly cover. Cut the remaining *quarter of butter* into pieces the size of a chestnut, and put them over the meat. Roll the remainder of the crust to fit the top. Make a curving cut in the crust and turn it back, that the steam may escape. Bake three hours in a brick oven. If baked in a stove oven, put on only two rims of crust and bake two hours.

MARCH

TREE WORK IN VERMONT

Maple cream pie in Vermont is like a unicorn. They are equally abundant in the modern world and equally tasty. When the sap flows, the sugar bushes churn in March and the houses put out their share of syrup and candy, maple pie seems to have been left behind. An occasional out-of-the-way diner will offer a slice of the "elusively flavored" pie, in the words of Florence Harris, with its silky custard and flaky crust, but it is mostly seen as a thing of the past, a relic of history and bygone days. Like a unicorn.

To look backward in history is something that can be done only at great peril. Things that now appear obvious about the past can be turned on their head when we shake off the blinders of the present perspective. Most Americans today imagine slavery as a legacy of the South, for example, in part because southern whites remained fiercely committed to slaveholding for so long and in part because southern whites chose to spark a war rather than divest of human chattel. But there is another view that New England did more than its share in conducting the British colonies toward slavery. Despite their rhetoric about liberty and conscience, Puritans bathed deep in the waters of hierarchy and lived lives in which conscience was severely constrained by culture. Everyone from swineherds to clergy to the king himself had a proper place in the Puritan order of things, and all were expected to know it. To violate one's station in life, to act mightier than one's birth, triggered a response from the authorities. For the average colonist in Massachusetts Bay, an "excess in apparell" was a crime, according to the sumptuary laws of 1651, and for man to wear "gold or silver lace, or buttons, or points at their knees, or to walk in great boots" was forbidden. For a woman to array herself in "silk or tiffany hoods, or scarves" was "intolerable." Defying the authority of clergy (the pinnacle of Puritan society) invoked the proverbial wrath of God. Or the Mathers. Whichever was worse.

In such a world, Puritans regarded slavery as just another shade of the social order. *The Body of Liberties* (1641), the first legal code in New England, authorized enslavement for "lawfull Captives taken in just warres, and such strangers as willingly selle themselves or are sold to us." Soon after, both Plymouth and Connecticut dove into the enslaving mire with both feet, agreeing to the return of runaway "servants."

A bright exception, that more tolerant alternative to theocracy, Rhode Island feinted in a more humane direction. In 1652, when few were enslaved in the region, the General Court ruled that "no black mankinde" could be held in bondage for more than ten years, after which they must be set "free, as the manner is with English servants." Seven years later, the court went further, prohibiting the importation of African captives altogether. This was comparative equality. But whatever intentions lay behind these statutes, neither was really enforced, and with the restoration of King Charles II and the issuance of a new charter, the laws became dead letters. Slavery picked up steam in little Rhody.

Like other British colonists, Rhode Islanders increasingly turned to Africa for their captive needs, and by the turn of the eighteenth century, they had outstripped their New England neighbors in zeal for the practice. While their plantations may not have been as grand as southern ones, the percentage of enslaved in Newport and South County nevertheless approached southern levels. By midcentury, nearly 10 percent of the colony's total population was held in bondage.

More notably, Rhode Islanders became leaders in transatlantic trafficking in captives, sending an average of eighteen ships per year into the triangular trade. This was a simple and lucrative scheme: import Caribbean sugar and molasses homeward, distill it into good New England rum, ship the rum to Africa to exchange for captives and sell the captives in the American south and Caribbean. When done, acquire more molasses and repeat. It was a perpetual motion machine, a triangle of sweetness, oblivion and death.

Before the American Revolution, Rhode Islanders were complicit in transporting nearly sixty thousand Africans to the New World, and in the years after, perhaps 60 percent of ships sailing from British North America to Africa left from its ports. Even New Englanders who stood apart from the trade profited from it, supporting slavery through sale of our region's vital products, from timber to beef, pork, salt cod, horses, osnaburg cloth, shoes and iron goods. From shipbuilders to distillers to the textile mills that outfitted the enslaved, the whole economy was shaped by slavery, directly and indirectly.

Even New England's piemakers felt the dead hand of slavery. An essential ingredient of pies, sugar, was virtually the symbol of the plantation system. Ruthless machines, these plantations were synonymous with brutality and depravity, as efficient at grinding slaves as they were at grinding cane. Their sheer efficiency ensured that eventually slavery would raise concerns. Even for an ordered Puritan mindset, plantations were just too much to ignore.

While antislavery sentiment grew at a glacial pace, many of the most insistent voices in the British world came from the Religious Society of Friends, the Quakers. Far from beloved by Puritans—who executed four Friends in 1659–61 for having the temerity to enter Massachusetts Bay—Quakers held that every individual had a spark of the divine within, an Inward Light, and many Quakers concluded independently that the Inward Light must animate Africans as well as Europeans, and women as well as men, giving rise to a strong antipathy for most forms of hierarchy. From this small seed, antislavery grew. Slowly.

So unlike Puritans in so many ways, the Society of Friends is organized into local meetings for worship ("Monthly Meetings"), which are, in turn, gathered into larger and essentially autonomous bodies known as Yearly Meetings, the most important of which were those in New England, Philadelphia and London. Unity and consensus are much esteemed, and since there are no ministers to guide Quaker Meetings, and no single overarching authority to enforce orthodoxy, it could take years for Friends to build consensus on controversial issues. Persuasion was key. Quakers did not awake one day realizing that slavery was an inherent evil, but members of Monthly and Yearly Meetings conversed doggedly with those who saw differently, moving cautiously at their own pace.

As much as any issue, slavery vexed Quakers. Even as some invested in the enslaved or traded in captives, others felt the need to live up to the calling of the Inward Light. Shocked by what he saw during a visit to the sugar colony of Barbados, Irish Friend William Edmundson vehemently condemned slavery as early as 1671, and separately, Friends in Germantown (1688) and Merion (1696), Pennsylvania, petitioned their Yearly Meeting to end "the traffick of men-body."

There were halfway approaches too, sadly. George Fox, one of Quakerism's founders and a fellow traveler with Edmundson in Barbados, witnessed the "sore Burden" of slavery there but stopped short of condemning masters, urging them only to imagine themselves in the place of the enslaved, treat them humanely and instruct them in proper gospel order. Wherever opposition to slavery was found among Friends, slaveholders in Meetings allied themselves as a conservative bulwark, advocating for gradual change to stave off abolition. It took generations of discussion between London, Philadelphia and New England to produce movement (and a movement) and to define what Friends would be. The pattern was consistent: "moral suasion" by individual activists led meetings to urge humane treatment, then to call for end the slave trade and, finally, to proscribe slavery itself.

Like Fox before them, the Philadelphia Yearly Meeting cautioned Friends in 1696 "not to Encourage the bringing in of any more Negroes" and demanded that "such that have Negroes be careful of them, bring them to Meetings, or have Meetings with them in their Families." Twenty years later, Chester Monthly Meeting convinced the Yearly to caution against slave trafficking, although the devil lay in the details. Cautions without consequences did little to dissuade the worst offenders, and many slaveholding Quakers simply ignored their Meetings' pleas.

Recognizing the problem, Quaker reformers turned up the heat in the 1740s and 1750s, arguing that slavery itself, not just the slave trade, was un-Christian and unacceptable. In particular, John Woolman's pamphlet *Some Considerations on the Keeping of Negroes* (1754) inspired Philadelphia not only to ban "the practice of Importing, buying, selling or keeping Slaves" in 1758 but also to bar members who traded in slaves from participating in business meetings. Slaveholders could remain Friends in good standing, to be sure, but from then on, their influence waned. Woolman played a crucial role in New England, too. While visiting Newport in 1760, he was distressed to find a Friend, Peleg Thurston, selling captives newly arrived from Africa right near the meetinghouse. He immediately shamed the New England Yearly into issuing a new query on slaveholding.

The bats came home to roost in London in 1761. Although too often disinclined to discipline slaveholders within its own Meetings, London Yearly mandated disownment (excommunication) for offenders, putting teeth behind abolitionist suggestions for change for the first time. In 1770, New England Yearly began to require members to manumit captives who were "of an age and condition suitable for freedom," and Philadelphia concurred in 1775, although slaveholders everywhere offered a steady diet of excuses, stalling tactics and outright refusals to comply. It was a painful process to move (or purge) slaveholders, but it was a process that began in earnest.

The timing was interesting. As Quakers stirred the language of liberty for the enslaved, non-Quakers were stirring the revolutionary rhetoric of political liberty for the colonies. During the American Revolution, significant numbers of non-Quakers began questioning slavery for the first time and were greeted with the same recalcitrance by their slaveholding peers. While other New England states systematically banned slavery, Rhode Island and Connecticut, where slavery was most firmly entrenched, vacillated. Rejecting immediate abolition in favor of gradual emancipation, they freed all persons born after March 1, 1784, but did nothing for those already in bondage. As a result, as late as 1840, Rhode Island still reported five persons held as slaves and Connecticut nearly one hundred.

As antislavery evolved, antislavery advocates in New England looked beyond ending their role as consumers of slaves to curtailing their role as middlemen in the system. This is the point at which parallel movements converge—the antislavery movement and the domestic manufactures movement—and where slavery met pie most directly.

The domestic manufactures movement began in the 1760s as a rebellious yawp against British taxation of essential imports such as sugar and textiles, and more generally, it was a plea to support American producers. The Revolution only sharpened desire for developing our native industries, hoping to win an economic independence to mirror the political. To demonstrate allegiance to their new nation, supporters clad themselves in homespun cloth rather than refined British textiles, and activists started "spinning schools" to promote home weaving among American women. To encourage local industry, learned societies offered prizes for the best woolens or best manufactured goods, and others rose to the challenge of spurring national education and science and a domestic literature. It was a movement that Americans embraced personally at home. Describing a typical New England Thanksgiving in her novel *Northwood*, Sarah Josepha Hale noted how the sideboard groaned under the weight of American products and homely American drinks such as currant wine, cider and ginger beer. "There were no foreign wines or ardent spirits," she insisted, the host "being a *consistent* moralist." Ironically, women in the Confederate South applied the same logic in spinning their own homespun movement during the Civil War, boycotting New England textiles to protest Northern "aggression" toward slavery.

If there was a single point where domestic manufactures and antislavery converged, it was sugar. Nearly all the sugar consumed in New England at the time was imported from the British Caribbean, and nearly all was produced on massive cane plantations using enslaved labor. In 1791, British antislavery workers lit on the idea of boycotting West Indian sugar as a way of exerting economic pressure on slaveholders, and British activists like William Fox soon expanded the boycott to rum (good New England rum), since it was both the product of slave-produced cane and a key commodity in the triangular trade. Rather than avoid sugar, advocates for the boycott proposed finding a substitute, which in Britain meant importing slave-free sugar from the East Indies. As activists spread the word through pamphlets and novelties such as sugar bowls emblazoned with the catchy slogan, "By Six Families using East India, instead of West India Sugar, one Slave less is required," the boycott spread. Within three years, more than 300,000 British families had switched to East India sugar, and New England, thanks largely to its Quakers, showed signs of joining.

Over here, our substitute for cane sugar would come not from Asia but rather from our abundant native maples. We had, it seemed, an answer to the problem of slavery in our own backyards. Replacing cane sugar with maple surprisingly did not originate with a New Englander but rather with Philadelphia's most renowned physician and a signer of the Declaration of Independence, Benjamin Rush. Becoming convinced that slavery was both immoral and incompatible with American liberty, Rush began his campaign in 1788 by publishing a small but influential tract on sugar maples, and he united soon thereafter with several Quakers to found the Society for Promoting the Manufacture of Sugar from the Sugar Maple Tree. Rush's aim was grand—no less than "to lessen or destroy the consumption of West Indian sugar, and thus indirectly to destroy negro slavery." It was almost poetical:

> *I cannot help contemplating a Sugar Maple Tree with a species of affection, and even veneration; for I have persuaded myself to behold in it the happy means of rendering the commerce and slavery of our African brethren in the sugar islands, as unnecessary as it has always been inhumane and unjust.*

As important as Rush was, it was a friend of his who took the cause to the next level. Renowned for his uncanny skill in holding two contradictory principles in mind at once, Thomas Jefferson, the steadfast slaveholder, briefly became a leader in arguing for the end of slavery through sweet cultivation. In Jefferson's hands, the moral argument against sugar would be welded to the economic desire to build up national self-sufficiency, yielding a potent two-for-one punch. After returning from an assignment

Horses ready for sugaring, Vermont, circa 1910. *Collection of the author.*

Sugaring in Vermont: a sugar house and maples set out with sap buckets, circa 1910. *Collection of the author.*

as minister to France in 1789, Jefferson blended Rush's antislavery sugar into the tea of his own independent yeoman farmers. Learning that the peak season for sugar production coincided with a time of year when northerners were otherwise idle, Jefferson was smitten with the thrift of it all and no less by the thought that sugaring required so little hard labor that women and children could ably assist. Our small, independent farmers would rescue the nation from the scourge of enslavement. Family economy and self-sufficiency dovetailed. Turning slack hours to profit, small farmers could satisfy their family need for sweeteners and, perhaps, produce excess for trade. It was a win-win-win proposition.

In June 1790, Jefferson overflowed with the spirit, writing to his friend Benjamin Vaughan that maples would yield high-quality sugar in high quantity by using "no other labor than what the women and girls can bestow...What a blessing to substitute a sugar which requires only the labour of children, for that which it is said renders the slavery of the blacks necessary."

Jefferson did more than talk. In November 1790, he purchased fifty pounds of maple sugar from Quaker merchants Edward and Isaac Pennington to test whether it was possible to refine a product equal to "the best [West Indian] muscavado," and he acquired maple seeds to start his own grove. Rush, too, was elated, announcing that Jefferson "used no other sugar in his family than that which is obtained from the sugar maple tree." The next May, when Jefferson and his friend James Madison toured the maple heartland of Vermont, he stopped in Bennington to encourage landowners to plant orchards of maple as they did apple. It was like a dream: witnessing efforts to develop the domestic production of olive oil and rice as well as maple sugar, Jefferson could almost taste a future free of slavery and free of commercial dependence on foreign powers.

Sadly, sugar maples and the Virginia climate did not mix well, and most of Jefferson's trees died a sad death. The search for slave-free sugar, however, lived on. Abolitionists like David Lee Child and his wife (and cookbook author) Lydia Maria Child added the noble sugar beet to the list of cane alternatives, but like Jefferson, their ideas worked better in their minds than in the ground. The Free Produce movement, led mostly by Quakers, took a broader approach, boycotting all goods produced with slave labor. Following the example of his intellectual forebears John Woolman, Anthony Benezet and Benjamin Lay, the Quaker saddle-maker Benjamin Lundy opened the nation's first "free produce store" in 1826. Challenged to locate sources of free produce in a world in which enslavement meant profit, Lundy scouted far and wide for goods free of the taint of slavery, seeking coffee from Haiti and tobacco from Canada, not to mention domestic maple sugar. Although the movement never captured the imagination of mainstream whites,

Lundy's fellow radicals, black and white, male and female, kept the torch burning. The moral choice was clear, as the Requited Labor Convention concluded in 1838: "As slaves are robbed of the fruits of their toil, all who partake of those fruits are participants in the robbery."

Even after the formal end of slavery, the maple continued to represent an alternative to a life of exploitation and dependence. Helen and Scott Nearing, the pacifists, anti-capitalists and advocates for simple living, made their living during the Great Depression from maple syrup and sugar, writing about their reverence for the tree. All at once, the maple represented economic freedom, a simpler way of life and a natural solution to the problems of the world attuned to ecological principles, and their call to act

Sugaring: collecting sap. *Photo by Roy Finestone, April 1977. Roy Finestone Collection, Special Collections, UMass Amherst Libraries.*

Calf and sugar shack, Northfield, Massachusetts. *Photo by I. Eliot Wentworth, 2013.*

and to live a principled life resounded with the minds of a generation of back-to-the-landers in the 1960s:

> [Maple trees] *are more than keen competitors for up to date factories, more than mere tissue-building machines or engines of living matter. From time immemorial…trees have been worshipped, held as sacred, and even depicted as living, important entities…. We want food? Fruits are there to be plucked from the trees, vegetables in the ground. But only because someone has labored to develop or help them grow. We want a home? Stone, sand, and timber cover the earth. We have only to dig, lift, pull, or hew.*

And so, early in March, when trees all across New England are tapped and the boil begins, it is an act of liberation to stumble inside, fresh from the snow and sit with a maple pie. For its past, and its promise for the future, this now-rare tradition reminds us that we have only to dig, lift, pull or hew to better the world.

RECIPES

Maple Syrup Pie (Social Union Cook Book, 1900)

One cup maple sugar, one egg, half cup milk, or cream, butter, size of a walnut, one tablespoon flour a bit of pepper, beat all until smooth and bake with two crusts.—Mrs. W.G. Simmons

Maple Apple Pie (Crockett, 1915)

For one pie: ¾ cup of lard, 3 or 4 good sour apples which have been pared and sliced, 1½ cups of flour, ½ teaspoonful salt, 1 cup maple sugar. Mix the lard, flour and salt thoroughly, add just enough cold water to work it lightly together; the less you handle pie crust the better it is—just enough to get it into shape to roll. Roll and put on plate, spread the apple and add the sugar. Bake in a moderate oven.

Maple Cream Pie (Wheel Cook Book, 1913)

Two cups scalded milk, one cup brown sugar or maple sugar, one-third cup flour, pinch salt, two eggs. Mix sugar, flour and salt, to this add heated milk; cook until smooth, then add yolks of eggs well beaten; cook for a few minutes until it thickens, then cook about a half hour. Make a meringue of the whites of the eggs and cover the top; brown.—Mrs. Darling.

Vermont Cream Pie (Harris, 1949)

Temperature: 450° F, then 325° F.
Time: 10 minutes, then 25–35 minutes.

unbaked pie crust
4 egg whites
1 tablespoon flour
½ cup maple sugar, shaved
2 cups hot cream

½ *teaspoon salt*

1 teaspoon vanilla extract or sprinkling of nutmeg

1. Line pie plate with pastry. Set in refrigerator until ready to be filled.
2. Beat egg whites until you can take up a spoonful.
3. Mix flour and sugar together.
4. Add egg whites. Fold in until well mixed.
5. Add cream to the mixture, then salt and vanilla or nutmeg.
6. Pour into pie crust. Set in a preheated oven and bake the required time or until a knife blade inserted in the center comes out clean.

APRIL

An American Euphemism

The theory that baseball causes global warming may be controversial, but it is based on close and careful observation. Each year, the natural experiment called spring training is replayed, coinciding with a time when New Englanders are losing their will over whether winter will ever end and whether we will need to readjust expectations for outerwear and inner peace. The results thus far are always the same: warm weather breaks out in Florida, and as baseball swings northward into the frozen lands, the warmth spreads with it until sometime in April, when Red Sox fans are able to divest themselves of just enough layers of coats and mittens to enter Fenway unfettered. Spring arrives. Baseball-induced warming may be no argument against league expansion, but it is a reminder that springtime is more than just a change of weather. It is a change of mindset and mood. In times past, before electricity and refrigeration changed the world of food preservation and eating, the arrival of fresh foods after a winter of pickled, canned and dried produce was something to cheer, a beacon for better times.

Spring in New England had its own, distinctive harbingers. Sugaring in March was a promise of life stirring, like marauding bears, ruby-throated hummingbirds or rivers of mud, but when it comes to pie, the surest sign of the season was the arrival of rhubarb. Pushing through to the sun as the last snows depart, like snow drops or crocus, rhubarb symbolized our reanimation. As the weather gathered nerve to warm itself, fitfully, hearty meat pies quickly ceded their privileged shelf in the oven to the bright hope of fresh fruit pies like rhubarb. Other fruits would have to follow. In the garden as in the kitchen, rhubarb was a visual relief. With enough oxalic acid to be toxic, the plant's deep green leaves defied the dulled earth and seasonal slush, framing a tart contrast with the artful ox-bloods and spring onion greens of its long, celery-like stalks. The ornamental virtues as much as the culinary ones made rhubarb a garden gem.

In April up north, with the Red Sox as backdrop and patches of snow still cowering in the north shade of the barn, my friend Rachel turned out a rhubarb pie to chase away the day. She is an experienced cook, excellent, but this was no delicate operation—ridding the stalks of toxic leaves and choking fibers, dicing them rough and tossing them into a crust with enough sugar to feed a continent of reawakened ants. It is hardly the stuff of haute cuisine. But Rachel is a crust master, and she knows that the details make the difference. Even where the filling corroded seams and boiled to the surface—a fearsome vision in mauve—her crust remained flaky and light. Somehow, when the pie emerged, its sweetness was restrained. There was texture, too. Entering raw into the fray, the rhubarb inside survived the long bake with integrity intact, resisting fork and molar long enough to demand acknowledgement. What made Rachel's pie stand out, though, was the insinuation of orange that came from an entire rind of zest and juice, a citrus complement to the rhubarb bite. Her friend Ben insisted that lemon made the pie even better, but there was no winning the argument. Rachel's rhubarb, a New England delicacy, was a product of two centuries of culinary history and perfect in the looming time of spring.

It may be no surprise, but like so many favorites of New England cuisine, rhubarb was an immigrant. Early Americans thought of the plant as an import from exotic Tartary, a region sprawling from China (its point of origin) to the Ukraine, and according to British horticulturist Henry Phillips, it made its way into western Europe as early as 1535. From ancient times, the plant was revered for the medicinal value of its roots, which were prepared as a purgative and laxative and as a powerful aid to maintaining the balance of bodily fluids. The difficulty of transport from central Asia made it among the costliest drugs in the European pharmacopoeia, particularly after a Russian czar asserted a monopoly on the trade, but its potency made it highly desired. In England, Phillips insisted that "all medical men acknowledge" its excellence in "evacuating bilious humours" and fortifying "the fibres of the stomach in the intestines." American physicians were equally sanguine. Daniel Whitney used rhubarb to evacuate "any acrid matter that may be

Slicing rhubarb. *Photo by I. Eliot Wentworth, 2015.*

Rhubarb stalks. *Photo by I. Eliot Wentworth, 2015.*

offending the bowels," and throughout the States, his colleagues prescribed its concoctions for any disease that called for depleting the system, including ague, diarrhea and dysentery.

A good purgative, though, did little to encourage thoughts of pie, and it took centuries for rhubarb to move from the medicine chest to the kitchen table. Only near the time of the American Revolution would a broader view of the vegetable emerge in the British world, spurred in part by horticultural societies seeking to advance agriculture. The Society for the Encouragement of Arts, Manufactures and Commerce, for example, issued gold medals in 1770 "For Introduction of the True Rhubarb Seed" and, in 1798, for innovation in cultivation.

When Americans finally took up the cause, they did so with gusto. America's best-known medical botanist, Benjamin Smith Barton, and one of its greatest horticulturists, Bernard M'Mahon, were partisans in a campaign to build an American national botany that could rival, or surpass, Europe's. For both men, the diversity of our climate, population and flora were a decided advantage, and in their minds, a great future would arrive when we learned to exploit the best of the New World to go with the best of the Old. Theirs was a species of reverse colonialism in which American farmers would exploit this continent's unique productions while adding to this bounty by importing the best plants of the Old World. We would remake our nation as a composite of people and crops, old and new.

In pursuit of this dream, Barton carefully studied Native American uses of plants, hoping to glean what he could in the way of new medicines or foods. In 1803, he expressed a wish that one day he might discover a rhubarb equivalent among them. Until then, he wistfully advised his fellow countrymen only that cultivation "ought to be attended to." More emphatically, in 1806, M'Mahon effused over rhubarb's potential. A radical émigré from Ireland, M'Mahon had a grand horticultural vision for the new nation so powerful that he convinced Thomas Jefferson to entrust him with rearing the irreplaceable plants and seeds collected by Lewis and Clark out west. When it came to the potential for rhubarb in America, M'Mahon asked rhetorically, "Shall we despair of bringing it to perfection, where soil and climate is perfectly congenial, and nothing wanted, but the enterprize of a few spirited individuals to make a commencement?" In American hands, he implied, rhubarb would achieve perfection. The campaign for rhubarb would be a small part of a grand project to propel the nation to an exceptional future, and it was this campaign by "spirited individuals" that formed the backdrop of New England's love for the pie of spring.

Having discovered that rhubarb was delectable when stewed with enough sugar to tame its tart tendencies, British cooks became industrious at smuggling it into puddings, sauces and tarts. Maria Rundell was an early convert. Deeply influential in America, Rundell's cookbook *Domestic Cookery* (1807) included one of the first published recipes for rhubarb pie, and through it, she may be as responsible as anyone for planting the rhubarb seed in American kitchens.

But for rhubarb to strut its stalks would require more than a few recipes; it would require a team of publicists. Although "America is blest with a favorable climate," a farmer named D.F. Ames wrote, and although we were "peopled by natives from all parts of the earth, who variously cultivate our various soils;" conservatism was stultifying. Despite all our national advantages, he insisted, "our markets are not so well supplied with fruit and vegetables as those of less favored lands." Progressive agricultural magazines such as the *New England Farmer* and *Genesee Farmer* took up the challenge, and in the late 1820s and 1830s, they pled with Americans to experiment and to try out new crops, new foods, new techniques and new ideas, rhubarb included, all in fulfillment of the new gospel of scientific agriculture and American values.

For promoters of rhubarb as food, the plant had a natural advantage: timing. The editor of the *Genesee Farmer*, Willis Gaylord, wrote that "at a time when other green articles for pies are difficult to be obtained," rhubarb would be there. Rhubarb was first out of the gate in spring, and for several weeks, it had few competitors in freshness. The prolific horticultural writer Edward Sayers called it "one of the best substitutes we have at an early season for green tarts," and Ames called it "a valuable plant" that had "the important recommendation of presenting itself for the table, when few others for a similar purpose are to be had." At a time of year when the only fruits available for pie were last fall's aging apples, Ames noted that rhubarb added a welcome zing, since an over-wintered apple "generally loses its flavor and becomes flat and insipid." The most avid supporter of the rhubarb may have been the "New-York Gardener," Agricola (publishing under a pseudonym), who gushed. "There is nothing more pleasant" in April than rhubarb, he wrote in 1824, "and physicians tell us there is nothing more healthy, than a frequent use of thrifty green vegetables." It relieved the dull similitude of winter and was a pleasure to the eye, the body and the taste. "[A]nd as variety alone can please," he wrote, "this plant should have a place in every kitchen-garden."

For Agricola, nothing could be better. "The majesty and beauty of the rhubarb," he claimed, "is not surpassed by any tenant of the garden."

Introducing an immigrant vegetable to unfamiliar Americans took patience and skill, beginning with learning how to cultivate it. Who first raised a rhubarb here is not recorded, but when living in London in 1770, Benjamin Franklin sent rhubarb seeds from the Society for Arts (from the gold medal winner, no less) to the great Quaker botanist John Bartram, and he sent more to the equally Quaker botanist Humphry Marshall in 1785. Neither man seems to have had long-term success, and in 1835, the *American Gardeners Magazine* ignored their efforts altogether, tentatively assigning credit for cultivating rhubarb to John Prince of Roxbury, a well-respected member of the Massachusetts Horticultural Society.

But cultivating the plant was only the first step in introducing it to a naïve nation, and further encouragement was needed. Agricola saw rhubarb as a prime example of "the slowness and difficulty with which every new vegetable finds its way to notice." In every country, he wrote, an innate "partiality to articles of customary culture" held many back from trying novel foods, and it was only "with hesitation and reluctance that our cooks attempt to dress new [vegetables], or to bring them to the table." Yet even when staring down the shackles of conservatism and its purgative reputation, Agricola was heartened by the progress rhubarb had already made. It was esteemed in England already, he noted, and in just sixty years, it had "spread from its native Tartarian mountains, or the hills of Thibet, to every part of the globe where horticulture is understood." In London, where tastes were a step ahead, it had gained so much that "thirty wagon loads of this article is sold every day."

Campaigners like Agricola and Gaylord introduced rhubarb to Americans by likening it to the familiar and much-loved apple. This fibrous vegetable with toxic leaves could easily daunt the uninitiated, but Gaylord stressed that it could easily be peeled, washed and used "in the manner of apples," remarking that if cooked properly with spices, the stalks would "make excellent pies, tarts, &c." It was as easy as apple pie. Like many promoters to come, Gaylord added that rhubarb would even charm the frugal-minded: as a perennial, it yielded year after year and was so productive that only a few plants would supply an entire family.

Campaigners realized, however, that merely launching the product would not be enough; it needed rebranding. "The true name of the plant," Agricola carped, did it no favors and had "in some instances prevented its culinary use…in order to prevent a previous nausea and disgust." To most

Americans, rhubarb equaled purgative. Fortunately, some unnamed proto-PR genius came up with the name "pie-plant" to divert attention. "Invented to disguise the somewhat painful associations of the generic name," as the British magazine the *Athenaeum* put it, this "American euphemism for rhubarb" did just enough to spackle over the old associations and convince New England cooks to adopt pie-plant into their pies. When the admirably frugal Lydia Maria Child complained in 1830 about the high cost of rhubarb pies because of the "enormous quantity of sugar" they required, the adoption was complete. If it was so expensive in a region so cheap, it was because it was so desired.

Ever since, pie-plant pie has been a bright presence of the New England spring, beloved enough to spawn dozens of variants. The early fellowship with apples remained strong for years, but cooks have paired it with almost any acidic fruit strong enough to withstand the stalky assertiveness, including gooseberry, pineapple and lemon. Rachel's orange-rhubarb had precursors as far back as Flora Haines Loughead's pie of 1891, and other cooks have tried to tame the rhubarb with custard or, like the Ladies of St. Mary's Guild of Grace Church in Providence, Rhode Island, with dollops of cream and meringue. Even odder mixtures have crept in, including a jam of rhubarb and fig (with raisins to boot) proffered by the African American corporate chef Rufus Estes in 1911.

Today, the most common variant of the pie revolves around a marriage with another sweet-acid fruit of the spring, the strawberry. The origins of this popular pie are obscure, but something was afoot at the turn of the twentieth century. Recipes for strawberry-rhubarb preserves were traded regularly for years, but in the pages of the *Boston Globe*, the pie sneaked in. Four years after a passing reference to strawberry-rhubarb pie in 1910, a recipe appeared under the byline, "B.B.," who declared the pie as "one of my mother's original recipes." Her version called for alternating layers of sliced rhubarb and strawberries—"the two flavors combine very well," she wrote. It was thickened with cornstarch and topped with butter and a dash of salt. Wherever it originated, New Englanders made strawberry-rhubarb their own, claiming the season for sweetness and a vision for a nation.

RECIPES

Rhubarb-Pie, New-England Style (Corson, 1885)

Make a good pastry, for which directions have already been given. Peel some garden rhubarb, or pie-plant, and cut it in small pieces; after lining the pie-plates with pastry, fill them with layers of rhubarb and sugar, and if a lemon is available use the grated yellow rind for flavoring; cover the pie, wetting the edges of the pastry to make them adhere; make several cuts in the top crust, and bake the pie in a moderate oven until both top and bottom crust are nicely browned; if the bottom of the pie cooks faster than the top, put a second plate under it when it is quite brown; if the top browns before the bottom is done, cover it with brown paper. Dust the top crust with powdered sugar after the pie is done, and use it either hot or cold.

Pie-Plant Custard Pie
(Ladies of the Congregational Church, Rutland, Vermont, 1891)

1 cup stewed pie-plant
1 cup sugar
1 tablespoonful flour
yolk of three eggs
small piece of butter

Bake under crust. Beat whites of eggs with three tablespoonfuls sugar; put into oven and brown.—Mrs. D.K. Hall

Rhubarb Cream Pie (Ladies of St. Marys Guild, 1905)

One cup stewed rhubarb (cold), 1 cup sugar, yolks of 2 eggs, 1 tablespoonful flour. Mix all together, and when crust is ready for oven add 1 cup milk and bake at once. Use the whites for meringue.

Rhubarb Pie (Strawberry-Rhubarb) (Greenbaum, 1919)

Make a very rich crust, and over the bottom layer sprinkle a large tablespoon of sugar and a good teaspoon of flour. Fill half-full of rhubarb that has been cut up, scatter in one-fourth cup of strawberries or raspberries, sprinkle with more sugar and flour, and then proceed as before. Over the top dot bits of butter and another dusting of flour. Use a good cup of sugar to a pie. Pinch the crusts together well after wetting them, to prevent the juice, which should be so thick that it does not soak through the lower crust at all, from cooking out.

Rhubarb Pie (Fredrika and Rachel, 2015)

Crust:
2 cups flour
1 teaspoon salt
1 cup Crisco

Break up Crisco into 8–10 pieces; chill in freezer. Mix together with other ingredients and 4–6 tablespoons ice water and chill in refrigerator for 30 minutes or so before rolling out.

Filling:
6 cups rhubarb
1 whole orange zested
2 tablespoon orange juice
1½ cups sugar
⅓ cup flour

Dot with butter and sprinkle bit of water on top. Place pie on lowest rack in oven at 450F. Bake for 15 minutes and reduce oven temperature to 350F, and continue baking for 40 to 45 minutes. Serve warm or cold.

MAY

FALSE PIES AND THEIR CONSEQUENCES

April Fool's Day has a single purpose in New England. It is an annual reminder of our regional motto, "I suspect." At a time when we are shaking off the complacency of a winter isolated by snow, the onslaught of childish pranks descends to remind us that everyone is suspect. It is our heritage to be suspicious, a heritage that descends from the English settlers who suspected even the holiest households of harboring witches and spreads out among the hundreds of small villages, where new arrivals will still be described as "new" twenty years later. It is a heritage strengthened each year when our famously fickle weather proves anew that the lamb of one day's spring can become a winter lion the next. Surface belies depth in New England, where even our beloved pies take part in subterfuge.

A family secret of mine, closely guarded until now, illustrates the lessons learned from deceitful pastry. Back in the dark days of the disco era, a young girl—we will call her Danielle—was entering kindergarten in a small Massachusetts city. Little did she realize that kindergarten was no place for idle play but rather an intellectual hothouse that would expose the dangers of relying on the surface meaning of words. On a chilly Thursday late in October, the story goes, young Danielle trekked to school in her best pink cardigan and blue scarf, a pair of floral gumboots keeping her feet dry. Like every other morning at Our Lady of Little Things, she and her classmates huddled onto a mat in the center of the room to await the relentless interrogation. Where is your nose, her teacher asked. What is your favorite color? What pets do you have at home? Here. Blue. A cat. The questions flew fast and furious until the teacher at last turned up the heat. What, she asked, is your favorite pie?

Like a bolt of lightning, the question struck little Danielle, already nervous about speaking out. The smallest child in the room and the shyest, she churned as her bolder classmates rattled off slice by slice of apple, cherry and blueberry, and she was awed by a redhead who distinguished herself by citing chocolate cream, earning a shower of knowing nods for her tact and sophistication. Yet underneath her cardigan, Danielle struggled. As her classmates answered confidently down the line, she wrestled with whether to join the chorus of berries and creams or go with her deepest instinct, her heart, the love of her young gustatory life. Summoning all her courage, she spoke truth to power. Danielle loved shepherd's pie.

There would be no knowing nods that day, only long peals of laughter, and young Danielle reddened to a cardigan hue when the teacher next door was summoned to hear her repeat the words "shepherd's pie." Although few of us remember how we learned what makes a pie a pie, Danielle would never again forget. No matter how you slice it, shepherd's pie is an awkward fit, a charlatan pastry, a forged check on the bank of pie. However much they vary in size and structure, pies are defined by their crust, either on top or below (or both), while the lowly shepherd's pie cowers beneath a formless froth of potato.

From its first appearance in the nineteenth century, the name shepherd's pie has been used for a humble dish of cold meats and mixed vegetables, typically graced with gravy and baked under a quilt of mashed potato. Scrupulous food writers will sometimes insist that the name should be reserved only for pies made with lamb or mutton—after all, shepherds are sheep herders—using the term "cottage pie" for its beefy counterpart. But the scruples of modern writers were not widely shared in the nineteenth century, and in fact, many cookbook authors indicated explicitly that the type of meat was moot: whatever one had on hand would do. This is New England comfort food at its most basic, a dish beloved despite (or because of) its unapologetic lack of refinement. Spice and similar adventures are foreign concepts, and if there is any sprucing up to do, it is seldom more than sculpting a few potato peaks to crisp up while baking or perhaps adding a second potato layer at the bottom. Shepherd or cottage, it is the potato exterior, not the fleshy interior, that makes the dish.

Given that the British and their descendants have savored meat pies since the Middle Ages, it may come as a surprise that the potato took so long to get with the pie game. Relatively speaking, potatoes are newcomers to British food—or, more accurately, New World–comers. Plundered from

Shepherd's pie (or, more accurately, a pâté chinois), Atkins Farms, Amherst, Massachusetts. A French Canadian version of shepherd's pie, the pâté chinois has a filling of beef and corn and little else. *Photo by I. Eliot Wentworth, 2015.*

South America by the Spanish conquistadors and imported to Europe late in the sixteenth century, potatoes were originally viewed as fit only for invalids, the Irish and the poor, which were close to synonyms. Only a long effort to gull the humbler sorts into accepting the easy-to-grow and reliable food—ugly, yes, but good for you!—enabled potatoes to ascend into the diets of the middle and upper classes and, eventually, into pies. Blazing the trail were cookbook authors such as William Salmon (1710) and John Nott (1723) whose taste for tubers was essentially a medieval blending of savory and sweet. Their potato pies were studded with almonds, pistachios, dates, candied citron peel, lemon and orange, to go with wine and sugar. Such combinations of sweet stuff and savory spud remained the norm for years. Near the end of the eighteenth century, the proprietor of a Scottish cooking school, Susanna MacIver (1789), offered a sweet "apple pie with potato" that included layers of fruit, sliced potato ("rather more apples than potatoes") and butter, topped with puff pastry.

But the potato's future lay at the savory end of the spectrum, not the sweet. The author of the most popular cookbook of the century, Hannah Glasse, offered an early version of a purely savory pie, mixing boiled and buttered potato with boiled eggs, pepper, white wine and nutmeg, while other writers mixed potatoes under the crust of meat pies, recognizing the potato's ultimate destiny. Precisely who first thought of replacing pie crust with potato, however, is difficult to discern, but there were two clear avenues toward that end. For one, the popular British author Maria Rundell (1807) and Massachusetts's own Mrs. Cornelius (1808) offered recipes for potato paste (i.e., pastry), in which flour was worked into mashed potato to make a rollable dough that could be treated like crust. Although both authors enjoyed great popularity, it is unclear whether potato paste did, too. The doyenne of American cooking, Eliza Leslie, included a recipe in her *Directions for Cookery* but alerted readers that the result was too heavy and "unfit for baking" once cooled. Potato paste was a dead end.

The second approach to housing the pie took off on cues from Salmon and MacIver, layering the ingredients and ensuring that potatoes came out on top. Rundell's "potato pie," for example, featured potato slices layered with "some mutton, beef, pork, or veal," leaving only a small step—swapping sliced for mashed—to complete the shepherd's circuit. That step involved an ethnic intervention: an "Irish stew" (or "hunter's pie") recorded by the best-selling British health reformer William Kitchiner (1821) featured mutton neck laid on and under a bed of mashed potato. Even more important for the American audience, New England's paragon of domestic perfection, Catherine Beecher (1846), followed with two recipes: a layered pie that featured beef, veal or chicken under a potato paste and a "potato pie" that closely resembled the noble shepherd—starting with a bed of mashed potatoes, Beecher laid cold meats and potato alternately before topping the whole with a final round of mashed.

With this, the path of the potato to the crown of a shepherd's pie was nearly complete. All that was needed was the name. Although the term "cottage pie" had been in use by 1791, according to the *Oxford English Dictionary*, shepherd's pie appears not to have broken through until perhaps 1854, when it was announced to the world as Scottish. Mrs. Williamson, a "confectioner and pastrycook" from Edinburgh, applied the term to a dish that included "cold dressed meat of any kind, roast or boiled," paired with sauce and "a little mushroom ketchup" and topped with a glorious mound of mashed potato. Williamson was quite precise: the topping must be smooth and notched on the edge, "the same as paste," and it must be baked "until the potatoes are a nice brown."

Ah, deceptive words. The shepherd's pie had retained its status as pie through a tortured journey through meat and paste. Under its varied names, shepherd's pie grew steadily in the New England imagination, passing through Beecher to the pages of Maria Parloa and the Boston Cooking School and onward into hundreds of cookbooks spawned by community groups and charitable organizations. Resonating with a regional penchant for thrift, shepherd's pie reveled in its reputation for economy, even as the meaning of *economical* evolved. For early writers like Cornelius and Rundell, household economy meant spending well while spending less, but as historians remind us, even the most central ideas of hearth and home changed as the Industrial Revolution gripped New England. To understand how, it may be better to look to the clock than the engine. Machinery may have powered the Industrial Revolution, but it took a workforce attuned to the regularities of a workday to make an industrial economy efficient, and it was a long, hard slog to get workers to accept the discipline of the clock. As a regimented and mechanized workplace supplanted the slower and more varied seasonal clock of agriculture, home economy followed suit, with time and resource efficiency becoming the watchwords of the kitchen. Shepherd's pie was a perfect fit for this new world, as Clara G. Brewer suggested in 1907, while still suiting the woman's role in caring for her family:

> *A lack of good management of "left-overs" contributes to waste. It is one thing to get them eaten under protest so that they just escape being thrown away; it is another thing to use the "left-overs" so skillfully as to make attractive and palatable dishes, and so save the expense of providing new food. If the family does not like hash, there is no merit in using cold meat in this way and having it eaten "at the point of the bayonet," when, as croquettes, or filling for an omelet, or in shepherd's pie, the dish would be relished and praised.*

Clever leftovers, deceptive in how they refashioned ingredients, were lauded by Fannie Farmer, who included cottage pie under the heading, "Ways of Warming Over Beef." Leftovers assumed an added urgency during the food shortages of the First World War, when waste became a matter of life or death. But it was the promised efficiencies of new technology as much as deception that propelled the leftover to its place in the New England heart. Bearing a name that evoked a simpler era of pastoral peace, shepherd's pie provided a deceptive sense of presence and past for this newfangled age. When the electric refrigerator first swarmed the American kitchen in the 1920s, it brought radical opportunities for both people and leftovers, and the companies that produced them aided and abetted a revolution in American taste. When still so new that most Americans could "scarcely realize the range of its possibilities," the refrigerator was touted by General Electric as "almost like having an Aladdin's lamp and not knowing the right way to rub it." By familiarizing themselves, women could unlock the refrigerator's magic and discover that it was nothing less than "a form of health and happiness insurance." Even bolder, Frigidaire hailed the machine in 1928 not only for its power in "preventing needless food spoilage and safeguarding health in hundreds of thousands of homes throughout the world" but also for the promise it held for reordering the family economy:

> *Frigidaire plays a definite role in the daily routine and management of the modern home. It is an integral part of the equipment that lightens household cares and contributes to the health, happiness and convenience of every member of the family. Proper refrigeration is an ever increasing necessity of the American home. For the rapid growth of population in cities and urban areas has brought dependence upon distant centers of food supply…. It is vitally important with this complex distribution of food that every home has proper refrigeration….* [Now] *it is possible to go away for the week and or even longer without considering food supply. And Frigidaire is an economy. Savings over former ice bills, needless good spoilage eliminated, and ability to purchase in larger quantities at reduced prices makes Frigidaire, the outstanding automatic refrigerator, one of the greatest essentials of the modern home.*

The age of refrigeration was an age in which women and families would be rescued from the limits of food availability imposed by time and place, and shepherd's pie—now an option for a "week or even longer"—became the symbol of this unbounded order, demonstrated in Frigidaire's brand-new "experimental kitchen."

Even more daring than the commercial producers were the home economists at Smith College, who included shepherd's pie in their experiments to find domestic efficiencies through community cooperation. Between 1925 and 1931, the college's Institute for the Co-Ordination of Women's Interests created a model Community Dinner Kitchen to test whether community cooperatives could lighten women's household burdens enough to allow them to pursue their own interests without sacrificing the "duties" of married life. Community kitchens might be either cooperative or proprietary, they argued, or might take the form of a tearoom, an association of home assistants or a training center, but in any formulation, they privileged a central site where meals were prepared cooperatively for distribution to families, saving time for all.

AND FARTHER NORTH

Shepherd's pie is not the only deceiver in the New England kitchen, and for those Down East it is not even the most famous. That would be the whoopie pie. There is no universe in which the whoopie pie can be considered an actual pie—it is an inverted impostor of frosting slathered between two layers of cake—but as a so-called pie, it has taken over the minds of northern New England. To say the least, the origins of the treat are hazy and hotly contested, and for reasons that defy logic, three states claim equally to be its natal home. Pennsylvanians invoke the Amish in nearly every version of their origin story, claiming either that an unnamed Amish woman exclaimed "whoopee!" at seeing her cakes come out of the oven or that Amish children (or sometimes men) did the exclaiming when finding a pie in their lunchboxes. Apparently, "whoopee!" is the go-to exclamation for the Amish, but whether or not this is so, the treat is popular in the Keystone State. Near Pittsburgh, a similar confection goes by the name gob, which only leads to the conclusion that steelworkers are less prone to exclamation.

Few New Englanders accept the Amish story, given its lack of serious evidence, and many point instead to the Labadie Bakery in Lewiston, Maine, which sold "whoopie pies" as early as 1925, or to the Berwick Baking Company of Roxbury, Massachusetts, which is said to have carried them before 1931. Whichever story or state one believes, the whoopie pie appears to be a product of the 1920s. The timing of its appearance may be connected to the famous Devil Dogs, the oblong but otherwise similar pastries produced by Drake Bakeries of Brooklyn that first appeared in 1923. One can certainly imagine a New England baker shouting, "Whoopee, I've infringed on a competitor's copyright, made it round instead of oval and renamed it a pie!"

Wherever the term originated, "whoopee" has a decidedly Jazz Age feel. As an interjection to express joy, the term was already in use by the 1860s, according to the *Oxford English Dictionary*, but by the 1920s, it had acquired the vaguely risqué and painfully hip overtones of flaming youth. Discussing the "slanguage" of America in 1929, the *Manchester Guardian* noted that "whoopee" was "applied to all varieties of unbridled revelry, usually containing joyous ingredients of wine, women, and warbling," and even the Boston Police Department got in on the act, forming "anti-whoopee" squads to keep watch on seedy hotels, nightclubs and dance halls for untoward activity. "Whoopee" was launched into stratospheric popularity in 1928 thanks to the boffo success of a musical comedy of that name, produced by Florenz Ziegfeld and starring the comedian Eddie Cantor. The play featured the Gus Kahn hit song "Makin' Whoopee," and two years later, it became a rousing Busby Berkeley film, one of Hollywood's earliest talking pictures filmed in color.

Although none of this rises to anything more than idle speculation, the rival states involved seem intent on digging in their heels when claiming paternity for the dubious pie. The rivalry between Maine and Pennsylvania, in particular, was already nearing a boiling point in the new millennium, when citizens in both states set up rival whoopie festivals to stake their claims, but in 2011, the clever machinations of Paul Davis drove the rivalry to unprecedented heights. A representative from Dover-Foxcroft, home to the Maine Whoopie Pie Festival, Davis already knew the Maine whoopie well, and with the urging of Amos Orcutt, president of the University of Maine Foundation and, more importantly, founder of the Maine Whoopie Pie Association, he decided to take action. Heading the pie-mad Pennsylvanians off at the pass in January 2011, Davis introduced a bill into the state legislature designating the whoopie pie as the state's official dessert, urging his fellow representatives to set aside their partisan preferences and unite behind pastry.

With support from the festival promoters and from bakeries large and small, the bill started off strong. But politics being what it is, the whoopie wave soon crashed on the reef of opposition. Citing the rise of obesity in the state, Representative Donald Pilon (D-Saco) lambasted the "frosting-delivering vehicles masquerading as food" in an effort to galvanize the opposition, and he was quoted as grumbling, "Whoopie pie, it's not even a pie…It's two pieces of cake with frosting in the middle." Knowing his audience well, the silver-tongued Pilon attempted to stick a fork in the bill by claiming that the whoopie pie was probably invented "in that den of iniquity to our south," Massachusetts. No sterner words are to be heard from a politician in Maine (or New Hampshire or Vermont or sometimes Massachusetts). Siding with the opposition, other politicians, and some ordinary citizens, huffed that Davis's "frivolous" bill was a waste of taxpayers' money.

This was front-page news in Maine, and even the stoic *New York Times* felt compelled to report the drama. Down south, Pennsylvanians reacted with sweet fury, organizing protests against Maine's "act of confectionery larceny" and building websites to "Save our whoopie." Nearly one hundred irate citizens gathered in Lancaster in the mid-February cold to claim the whoopie for their own, one person carrying a sign reading, "Give Me Whoopie, or Give Me Death," as if the two were mutually exclusive. From his perch in Maine, Orcutt thoroughly enjoyed the furor, suggesting to the *New York Times* that Pennsylvanians are "somewhat deprived because they don't have lobsters and they don't have the wild Maine blueberry, so they're clinging on to this whoopie pie."

But more serious opponents rose up in Maine when the all-powerful blueberry lobby rallied around their antioxidants to force Davis into a concession. In March 2011, the Maine legislature voted 107 to 34 to designate the whoopie pie—charmingly described as "consists of two chocolate cake-like rounds surrounding a white cream filling"—as the state treat, while the blueberry pie would enjoy the distinction as state dessert. Although this might be considered a political compromise for the ages, Governor Paul LePage symbolically refused to sign the bill, claiming that it wasn't a priority. Lacking his signature, it nevertheless became law.

Nearly five years later, Davis still recalled the raft of "interesting" phone calls he received from Pennsylvania and the controversy that the pastry stirred Down East, but he remains adamant that the act he sponsored was "good for our state economically." Whoopie pies infect nearly every corner of Maine and have spread throughout New England. Dozens if not hundreds of the state's bakeries make them, as many as 100,000 per year, and the festival in Dover-Foxcroft pulls in between four and six thousands visitors per year, a huge economic boost in a small town. Pennsylvanians have not given up their claims, of course, but they have lost the initiative. With its origins clouded and its name deceptive, the whoopie is all Maine's.

RECIPES

Shepherd's Pie (Parloa, 1880)

One quart of any kind of cold meat, eight large potatoes, one small onion, one cupful of boiling milk, salt, pepper, and nearly a pint of gravy or stock, thickened with one table-spoonful of flour. Season the meat and put in a deep earthen dish. Grate the onion into the gravy, and pour over the meat. Pare, boil and mash the potatoes. Add the salt, pepper and milk and one table-spoonful of butter. Cover the pie with this, and bake gently half an hour.

Cottage Pie (Warren, 1881)

In the bottom of the pie-dish put a good layer of nicely minced mutton or beef, season to taste, add an onion chopped fine, cover with mashed potatoes, and bake in a sharp oven half an hour, or until the potatoes are well browned.

Cottage Pie No. 1
(New York Mayor's Committee on Food Supply, 1915)

Mix any left-over meat with a white sauce of some meat gravy and put in a baking dish. Take any left-over vegetables and mash them with a little milk. Spread this over the top of the meat and then bake in the over until brown.

JUNE

Washington and Lafayette
Visit Boston

Walking into the Parker House on a summer day is like walking into history. Outside the front door, the Freedom Trail scuttles with tourists on their way to Kings Chapel or the Granary Burial Ground or the Old State House, all just steps away, but inside everything is vertical. The enormous vault of the reception space and the scale of its marble and wood-carved expanse draw the eyes upward to a grand past, and from the windows of the restaurant looking out over Old City Hall, you can feel the weight of power.

We had come to try out the signature dish at the Parker House: the Boston cream pie, a luxurious treat served hundreds of times per week. It is a tiny powerhouse of its own. The toasted almond on its sides and an impeccable chocolate coating with spider-lace tracings in white create a counterpoint to the succulent cake and decadent cream. It is quite a performance, though not nearly the performance involved in calling it a pie. This is one addled dessert, one unable to confess that under all that ganache it is a cake. But this inability to tell cake from pie is part of its all-too-vertical history. As the father of our country might have said, I cannot tell a pie.

Rehashing the history of the American Revolution was a high art in early America, and Americans seldom skipped an opportunity to re-experience whatever made them exceptional and to reimagine why. By the 1820s, however, the tone had shifted, and the story of independence took on a sharp new insistence as realization set in that direct memories of the Revolution, and the Revolutionary generation itself, were rapidly fading. As our Patriots

Parker House, Boston, Massachusetts. *Photo by Detroit Publishing Company, circa 1900. Library of Congress, Prints and Photographs Division.*

died off, it seemed possible that everything we had achieved as a nation would pass away, too—the people, the values, the unity of purpose. Two events, more than any others, played into the concern: the American tour of George Washington's confidant and compatriot the Marquis de Lafayette in 1824–25 brought tears of nostalgia and remembrance, while the death of Thomas Jefferson and John Adams on the same day in 1826—July 4, no less—brought tears of grief.

Lafayette's visit was a sensation. Stoked with patriotic fervor, towns vied to outdo one another in appreciation and ostentatious displays of affection, and wherever he traveled, the marquis was greeted with parades, speeches, theatricals and throngs of ordinary citizens. Every evening he was feted by the political and social elite at lavish dinners and extravagant balls, such as the one in Boston, where he was assured by the great orator Edward Everett that "in all America there is not a heart which does not beat with joy and gratitude at the sound of your name." All the small things the marquis touched—the ribbons, bows, banners, place-cards, cockades and the napkins that graced the tables—became prized souvenirs not only of the visit but also, seemingly, of the Revolution itself. Memories persisted long after Lafayette was gone. In the fading lights of independence, Americans set out on a wave of new civic memorials, installing heroes permanently on public squares and commons for all to share. If George Washington had never slept here before, he surely did then.

The patriotic retrospect continued into the 1830s, when a handful of New England cookbook writers paid homage to our founders. Eliza Leslie may have started the trend with a recipe for Lafayette gingerbread, a spiced confection that toured the pages of her *Seventy-five Receipts* (1830). For understanding the lineage of the Boston cream pie, however, the Lafayette cake mattered more. In 1845, Ann H. Allen, author of a temperance cookbook with the evocative name *The Orphan's Friend*, honored the marquis with a recipe featuring "Savoy biscuit" (a deathly sweet sponge cake) baked in straight-sided pans. Allen's novel twist was to slice each cooled cake into quarter-inch-thick discs, spread them on top with jam or jelly and stack them into a layer cake of three or four tiers. In the grand manner of American publishing before copyright killed the fun, other cookbooks adapted or stole Allen's recipe and sent it on its own special tour through the culinary counties.

It was not long before Washington joined his old comrade in cake. Nodding to her Revolutionary heroes, Leslie's *Directions for Cookery* (1840) included a fairly typical recipe for Washington cake, a boozy, buttery fruitcake full of raisins and nutmeg, fortified with a good jolt of wine or brandy and a dash of rose water. Leslie promised that if "wrapped in a thick cloth, this cake will keep soft for a week"—with enough alcohol, who wouldn't? Washington was not just rich—he was durable. Washington and Lafayette even appeared together as cakes: one of James Beard's

Above: Mixing the egg and flour. *Photo by I. Eliot Wentworth, 2014.*

Left: Spry Shortening advertising booklet, circa 1940. *McIntosh Cookbook Collection, Special Collections, UMass Amherst Libraries.*

Dessert Magic . . . DOZENS OF DIFFERENT
DESSERTS CAN BE MADE FROM EACH OF THE FOUR
GOOD LUCK FLAVORS AND GOOD LUCK PIE CRUST

Left: Good Luck Pie Company advertising brochure, circa 1930. *McIntosh Cookbook Collection, Special Collections, UMass Amherst Libraries.*

Below: French meat pie. Burgundy Brook Café. *Photo by I. Eliot Wentworth, 2014.*

A classic New England chicken pie swimming in gravy and with fissures in the top crust. *Photo by I. Eliot Wentworth, 2014.*

Slice of rhubarb pie. *Photo by I. Eliot Wentworth, 2015.*

Strawberries awaiting their crusty fate. *Photo by I. Eliot Wentworth, 2014.*

Lloyd J. Harriss advertisement depicting George Washington crossing a river of cherry pies. The image is a spoof on Emanuel Leutze's painting of Washington crossing the Delaware, 1947. *Library of Congress Prints & Photographs Division.*

Wild blueberries and raspberries, New Salem, Massachusetts. *Photograph by I. Eliot Wentworth, 2014.*

Katya's Very Berry Pie (blueberry-raspberry). Allen's house, Royalston, Massachusetts. *Photograph by I. Eliot Wentworth, 2014.*

Minute Tapioca advertisement, circa 1935. *Beatrice McIntosh Cookbook Collection, Special Collections and University Archives, UMass Amherst Libraries.*

Right: "Woman Holding a Pumpkin." *Photo by Frank Waugh, circa 1925. Frank A. Waugh Papers (FS 088), Special Collections, UMass Amherst Libraries.*

Below: An extraordinary apple pie using local apples—one of the best pies in New England. Bashista Farms, Southampton, Massachusetts. *Photograph by I. Eliot Wentworth, 2015.*

Cooling racks with pies fresh from the oven. Granny's Pie Factory, East Hartford, Connecticut. Granny's has a wide range of high-quality pies, geared for the wholesale market and fundraising. *Photograph by I. Eliot Wentworth, 2015.*

A flaky crust in side view. Granny's Pie Factory. *Photograph by I. Eliot Wentworth, 2015.*

Pecan pie crusts ready for filling. Granny's Pie Factory. *Photograph by I. Eliot Wentworth, 2015.*

Newly made pumpkin pie ready for sale. Granny's Pie Factory. *Photograph by I. Eliot Wentworth, 2015.*

Left: Pressing out the crust. Granny's Pie Factory. *Photograph by I. Eliot Wentworth, 2015.*

Below: Pie counter. Rice Fruit Farm. *Photograph by I. Eliot Wentworth, 2015.*

Opposite, top: Fruits of the forest pie (apple, strawberry, blueberry, raspberry and mixed fruit). Proof that mixed fruit pies can be as good as the single fruit. Rice Fruit Farm. *Photograph by I. Eliot Wentworth, 2015.*

Opposite, middle: Bird's-eye view of the fruits of the forest pie. Rice Fruit Farm. *Photograph by I. Eliot Wentworth, 2015.*

Opposite, bottom: Pies for sale at the Williamsburg General Store, Williamsburg, Massachusetts. *Photograph by I. Eliot Wentworth, 2015.*

HOMEMADE
RASPBERRY PEACH
PIE
SMALL $7.99

Above: A small raspberry-peach pie from the Williamsburg General Store. *Photograph by I. Eliot Wentworth, 2014.*

Left: *Corn Products Cook Book*, circa 1920. *Beatrice McIntosh Cookbook Collection, Special Collections and University Archives, UMass Amherst Libraries.*

Maple-walnut pie. Chelsea Royal Diner, West Brattleboro, Vermont. *Photograph by I. Eliot Wentworth, 2015.*

The indescribable strawberry-rhubarb pie. Centerville Pie Company, Centerville, Massachusetts. *Photograph by I. Eliot Wentworth, 2015.*

Left: Apple pie, another of the best of New England. Petsi Pies, Somerville, Massachusetts. *Photograph by I. Eliot Wentworth, 2015.*

Below: A classic slice of New England blueberry pie. Centerville Pie Company, Centerville, Massachusetts. *Photograph by I. Eliot Wentworth, 2015.*

Today's version of the original Boston cream pie. Omni Parker House restaurant, Boston, Massachusetts. *Photograph by I. Eliot Wentworth, 2015.*

Pies for sale at the Centerville Pie Company. *Photograph by I. Eliot Wentworth, 2015.*

Cherry crumb pie. Petsi Pies. *Photograph by I. Eliot Wentworth, 2015.*

Sealing the edge of strawberry hand pie with an egg wash. *Photograph by I. Eliot Wentworth, 2014.*

favorite cookbook authors, Mrs. Thomas Crowen (1846), included both Washington cake and Lafayette cake.

Thus reunited, our Revolutionary brothers became honored guests at the New England table and were soon joined by their confused heir, the Washington pie. One of the more popular desserts of nineteenth-century New England, Washington pie may have borne Washington's name like the cake, but it had Lafayette's substance. This clever but perhaps unintentional sleight of hand may be attributed to Mary Hooker Cornelius, a native of Connecticut and wife of a noted missionary to the Cherokees. After including a classic Washington cake in the first edition of her *Young Housekeeper's Friend* (1846), Cornelius added a "Jelly-cake, or Washington Pie" to the much-revised edition that appeared two years later that thereafter became the pattern on which most Washington pies would be made. She dropped the Washington cake from later editions as the pie grew in stature.

With so much cake and so much pie, so much Washington and Lafayette, things could get confused. While a classic Washington pie contained a jelly layer—usually raspberry or strawberry when specified—and a few punctilious cooks like Fanny Farmer recommended dusting the top with powdered sugar, there was considerable variation in the cake and filling. Mrs. Putnam's Cornelius-like Washington pie was easily recognizable, for example, although she added saleratus and made her jelly layer "as thick as the cake," and her neighboring Lafayette pie (not cake!) was not much more than a sponge cake. But she followed these two recipes with a "filling for the above" made of custard. Other oddballs suggested filling with figs or stewed apples. In whatever form, the elegant Washington pie found an appreciative audience in Victorian America and became a staple of New England cookbooks for decades, even lending its name to the shallow, straight-sided pans in which it was baked.

By the Civil War, Washington pie had spread far enough that Colonel Charles C. Knott of the 176th New York Infantry relished it while being held as a prisoner of war in Texas. As Knott recalled, while being held at grim Camp Ford near the town of Tyler, he came up with the idea of lifting his men's spirits as the holidays approached by putting on a grand supper featuring the best of home cooking. Let out on parole to gather what they could, Knott and his comrades set out a holiday feast with prominent pies. Chicken pie, mince pie and pumpkin pie started it off, but the grand climax, Knott wrote, "was one of the efforts of genius sometimes called 'jelly-cake,' sometimes 'Lafayette cake,' sometimes

'Washington pie.' It was some eighteen inches in diameter, and four or five inches thick (the exact size of our dodger pot), a beautiful brown on the outside, and a rich golden yellow within, and when cut was seen to be divided by strata of tempting jelly."

A too-obvious staple at Washington's Birthday dinners, the pie could be found year-round as a special treat. Like any good thing, there was backlash, too. In the *Boston Globe* for August 1, 1889, a poet of ill repute took on the Washington pie:

The mighty name of Washington,
What vandal dared ally
With this malign monstrosity
That's neither cake nor pie?

A messy, mucilagious
Pestiferous compound, why
Should language hold such libel bold
Upon both George and pie?

'Twas Satan, sure, who, envious
Of his renown so high,
Evolved this vile viscidity,
The pater patriae's pie.

The shades of all the patriot dead
May well arise and say
Their curses 'gainst the blasphemy
Embodied in this pie.

O sisters of the Cooking School,
Your guilt you can't deny,
How could you, and cold-bloodedly,
Promulgate such a pie?

O sisters, tho' we every law
Of hygiene defy,
Let us sit down with emphasis
On George's so-called pie.

Ay, sisters, let us sit us down!
Tho' brothers who may try—
At picnics, say—the little trick
Of sitting upon pie.

Especially the pestilent
Kind that we here decry,
In spite of all their manliness
May be attached to pie,

Be sure tho' they love Washington,
to hostelries, they'll hie
And while they toast his name, they'll drink
Damnation to his pie.

What other pie could propel poets to such linguistic heights?

While Lafayette returned from France as a jelly-filled pie, another Frenchman was leaving his stamp on Boston cuisine. In 1855, Bostonian Harvey D. Parker purchased a property near the corner of School Street and Tremont with the intention of opening the nation's most elegant hotel. It was "an elegant edifice, of pure white marble," as a tourist's guide remarked, "and one of the foremost hotels in the country. The 'Parker House' is too well known to need a single word in its commendation."

For much of the nineteenth century, hotels were not simply places to stay but rather centers for socializing for the respectable classes (and sometimes the not-so-respectable). Parker's genius was his ability to make the Parker House the grandest statement of all for what a modern hotel could be. First off, he knew that the trick to real estate was location, location, location, situating his hotel in the heart of the city's political district, just down the hill from the statehouse and directly across School Street from city hall. Not coincidentally, this hotel that looked the part of a powerful edifice quickly emerged as a center for backroom politicking and power brokering.

Parker's hotel was a clever performance in other ways, too, and he immediately recognized that the food he served would have to match the elegance of construction. Upscale restaurants were a relatively new phenomenon in nineteenth-century America, with hotels being the epicenter of fine dining. But all that was beginning to change in the 1850s as American culinary entrepreneurs were becoming more ambitious, so Parker needed a grand gesture to stand out. With French cuisine viewed as the hautest of haute, Parker reportedly imported a French chef named M. Sanzian in 1855 at the princely salary of $5,000 to run his kitchens.

Sanzian brought instant respectability to the Parker House, and in a myth told and retold over the years (without much evidence, mind you), he was said to have introduced an especially elegant "Chocolate cream pie" to the world in 1856 that consisted of rounds of buttery sponge cake separated by a rum-infused cream and topped off with a layer of glossy chocolate fondant and—the chef's touch—a layer of sliced almonds on the sides. The recipe has evolved little over the years and remains the signature dish in the Parker House kitchen (its rolls excepted).

This *specialité d'hotel* gradually leaked out to other New England cooks, or at least to those adventurous enough to risk it. In 1886, Mrs. D.B. Moore of Biddeford, Maine, riffed on Sanzian's idea, incorporating chocolate into the custard layer of a chocolate cream pie, and more professionally, Maria Parloa, one of the original instructors at the Boston Cooking School, introduced a chocolate cream pie to her *Kitchen Companion* (1887) that threw Sanzian's chocolate jacket over the cake and custard. Interestingly, the very next recipe in Parloa's cookbook is for a classic Washington pie, proving that peaceful coexistence is possible in our time. Other variations on the theme followed, using pound cake instead of sponge; tweaking the texture with new products like baking powder (which was invented at nearly the same time as the Boston cream pie); playing infinitely with the mix of custard, cream and icing; and, perhaps most commonly, omitting the chocolate. Just to confuse matters, other chocolate cream pies sprang up around the same time, and these were verifiably pies—as much as we know what pies are, that is.

The name Boston cream pie adhered to the dessert as early as 1875, when a recipe appeared in the *New York Times* that featured a slather of lemon- or vanilla-tinged custard between layers of sponge. Lacking in chocolate, it resembles a Washington pie as much as Boston cream. Both pies peaked in popularity after 1900, when the *Washington Post* ran a scathing exposé about the profusion of names and recipes entitled "What Constitutes Mysterious Washington Pie?" In this subtle roman a clef, a fictional Down Easter begins by asserting that Washington pie referred to a three-layer cake with jelly between, to which an equally fictional westerner retorted, "But that's not Washington pie…that's simply layer cake. Washington pie, though, is something like cake, and in between is a creamy filling made of eggs and milk and sugar and a little flavoring. And you put powdered sugar on top." Predictably, the self-proclaimed expert in the group, a Bostonian, intervened to insist that what the woman described was Boston cream pie and that Washington pie did not exist. "Do you think it fitting to name a pie after an important historical figure?"

Aimed at the home cook, simplified versions of Boston cream sprang up in Miss Parloa's wake, shared through newspapers and community cookbooks, and commercial bakers entered the field, too. Convenience increasingly caught hold with this time-consuming dish. The high-volume baker Drake's was an early entrant in 1928, encouraging cooks making Boston cream pie to purchase premade "Drake's Handy Layer Cakes" and simply spread them with the right stuff. By the 1950s, prepackaged mixes sold by companies such as Betty Crocker and Duncan Heinz were ensuring that even the least skilled home cook could connect to the tradition.

The Parker House churns on as a premier hotel in Boston, perhaps the nation's oldest, and its kitchens have continued to pump out its revolutionary products. Had you visited the Parker House in 1912 or 1913, there is a chance that your Boston cream pie might have been made by the Vietnamese independence leader Ho Chi Minh while he was employed there as a pastry chef, and in the 1940s, your table might have been bussed by Roxbury native Malcolm Little before he changed his career and name to Malcolm X. The pie with Revolutionary beginnings and tangled heritage is now officially part of Massachusetts history, thanks to some lobbying by John Hickey's civics class at Norton High School in December 1996. "His idea," the *New York Times* reported, "was to come up with a noncontroversial bill and see if Norton students could get it passed." Massachusetts politics being what it is, the exercise meant taking on the Toll House cookie lobby, which scoffed that the "pie" was not a pie at all, and both the pumpkin pie and Indian pudding cartels felt they had something to say about state desserts, as did the health-conscious, who ignored the rest. In the end, the persistent kids from Norton won out: the state legislature passed General Law ch.2 §41 in November 1996, and at a ceremony situated around a forty-seven-pound behemoth of cream and chocolate, the Boston cream pie was declared "the official dessert or dessert emblem of the commonwealth."

RECIPES

Jelly-Cake, or Washington Pie (Cornelius, 1848)

Make cup cake, and when the ingredients are well mixed, spread it upon round shallow tins, three table-spoonfuls to each tin. It will bake in ten or fifteen minutes; then turn it upon a hair sieve, the under surface uppermost. While it is warm, spread upon it raspberry jam, currant, or other jelly; then lay the second sheet of cake upon it, the underside next to the jelly. If you wish to make several alternate layers of cake and jelly make the sheets of cake very thin; one large spoonful of batter will be enough for each tin."

Chocolate Cream Pie
(Ladies of the Second Congregational Church,
Biddeford, Maine, 1886)

One-third cup butter, one cup sugar, one egg, one cup milk, one-half teaspoon soda, one teaspoon cream of tartar, two even cupfuls of flour. Bake in three layers.

Filling.—One pint milk, one egg, one tablespoonful corn starch, one-half cup sugar, one-half teaspoonful vanilla, one square chocolate. Boil milk and the other ingredients all beaten together, melting chocolate. Frost if you like with frosting made of one cupful of sugar, one-half cupful of milks, a very small piece of butter, a little chocolate, boiled three minutes.

Chocolate Cream Pie (Parloa, 1887)

This is made in three parts—first the cake, then the cream, and finally the icing.

To Make the Cake.—Beat half a cupful of butter to a cream, and gradually beat into it one cupful of powdered sugar. Beat two eggs till light, and then beat them into the sugar and butter. Add half a cupful of milk and two level cupfuls of sifted flour, with which has been mixed a teaspoonful and a half of baking-powder. Beat this mixture quickly and vigorously, and pour into four deep tin plates that have been well buttered. Spread the batter evenly in the plates, and bake in a moderate oven for a quarter of an hour. Carefully remove the cakes from the tins, and put them in earthen plates.

To Make the Cream.—Beat together the yolks of two eggs, one table-spoonful of flour, and two table-spoonfuls of sugar. Put a cupful of milk into a double-boiler, and when it boils, add the beaten mixture and half a salt-spoonful of salt. Stir constantly until the mixture becomes smooth; then cover, and cook for fifteen minutes, stirring frequently. On taking from the fire add half a teaspoonful of vanilla extract.

To Make Chocolate Icing.—Mix six table-spoonfuls of grated chocolate and half a cupful of powdered sugar. Beat to a stiff, dry froth the whites of those two eggs whose yolks were used in making the cream, and gradually beat into them a cupful of powdered sugar and a teaspoonful of vanilla extract. Put the mixture of chocolate and sugar into a small frying-pan, and add two table-spoonfuls of water. Stir over a hot fire until smooth and glossy. Beat this cooked mixture into the mixture of egg whites and sugar.

Spread two of the cakes with the cooked cream, and spread a thin layer of chocolate icing over the cream. Place the other two cakes on top of the first two, and spread the remainder of the icing over them. Let the pies stand for at least two hours before serving.

Boston Cream Pie
(First Congregational Society, Unitarian, Chelmsford, 1949)

Make two layers of hot milk cake and fill with your favorite filling.
Top with Richmond Chocolate Frosting.

½ cup sugar
1½ tbsp. cornstarch
1 ounce sq. chocolate (shaved)
pinch salt
½ cup boiling water

1½ tbsp. butter
½ tsp. vanilla

Mix sugar, cornstarch, chocolate, and salt. Add boiling water and cook until thick. Add butter and remove from stove and add vanilla. Cool.—Mrs. Lawrence A. Litchfield.

JULY

CHERRY ON THE DOORSTEP

The most ephemeral fruits of the year are delivered in the warmth of summer, when long sunlight bastes the world in perfection. New England favorites like raspberries, blackberries, whortleberries and gooseberries ripen to the clockwork, arriving in brief flurries as the days begin to shorten. The span is briefest for cherries. When our ancestors spoke of "cherry week" at the market, they meant it. Three weeks in June and July are near the upper limit for a harvest, and rains can make it shorter, or birds, when they are more diligent than the orchardist. Forget an apple for a week or two and it will cling, ripe or riper; forget a cherry and a crow steals it away.

Every pie in the New England calendar aspires to royalty, and a few attain it. Having thrown off the imperial yoke 250 years ago, we now revere pies instead of princes. We are a pie-loving culture, a stretch of the country where the love for savory meats coexists with the love for fruit. And among all the many varieties, cherry stands out as one of the most beloved. In tree as in pastry, it is loved for the grace of new green leaves and near-black bark, for an effusion of floral color in early spring and for the way the fruit delivers a helix of sweet and tart to the tongue. Each part played, each essential. When not cutting down mythical trees, George Washington was said to adore the cherry pie, more than almost any other, although the recipe for sweetbread pie that appears in Martha's cookbook calls his fidelity into question. Regardless of what a wayward Virginian thought, for many in New England the sour cherry pie will always evoke the lush green heat of summer and the passing of an instant.

It may be surprising, then, that American cookbook authors show relatively little interest in the regal standard. Cherries were versatile enough to slip into cakes and puddings, and they made oceans of cherry water, wine and brandy, but as pies, they barely whisper. To be sure, this is a venerable pie. Culinary historians have noted that sweet fruit pies were sought after in the Renaissance and swelled in popularity during the reign of Queen Elizabeth, who was said to be partial to cherry pie. William Salmon's recipe from 1710 is as good a representative as any of the ancient genre, slight on sugar and comparatively delicate in spice. Even when extravagant cookery was valued, cherry remained a simple pie, and Salmon did little to expand its boundaries. A half century later, Hannah Glasse had even less to say than Salmon, advising her cooks simply to "make a good crust" and "throw sugar at the bottom" before laying in the fruit and sugar. Maria Rundell was no less terse but bolder in insisting that a cherry pie "should have a mixture of other fruit; currants or raspberries, or both." No cerise would go solo in Rundell's kitchen. Yet for most who followed, Rundell was whistling in the wind: cherry gloried on its throne alone, and perhaps it was this that explains the silence of the cooks. So many small and ephemeral fruits were essentially interchangeable as fillings for pie—raspberry, gooseberry, blackberry—that there was no need to repeat instructions if all that changed was a prefix or a rhyme for berry.

Baking a cherry pie may have required no outstanding effort, but for commercial bakers, the ease of baking did not translate into ease of sale, and as cities swelled, new opportunities for marketing baked goods swelled with them. As an early home to the Industrial Revolution, our region saw its dark satanic mills spawn many a city, titrating the population and grime into ever higher concentrations. This urban cauldron had an immediate impact on how people ate by simultaneously removing them from the places where those foods were raised and exposing them to wider cultures, foods and tastes. But cities also opened the door to convenience: prepared foods may or may not have been essential in urban kitchens, but in a city, they could easily be found and could even be delivered right to home.

Many Americans over the age of fifty—and some younger—remember home dairy delivery. In the town where I was raised, the milkman arrived each week to leave bottles of milk, a pound of butter or a dozen eggs in an insulated box on the porch. Fondly held as they are, such memories represent only the pale tail of a much deeper phenomenon reaching back to at least the 1860s. With few in the city owning their own cows or slaughterhouses, dairy and meat producers began direct delivery of their perishable goods

Johnson's Bakery delivery truck, circa 1925. *Collection of the author.*

to customers to gain a competitive edge. The pitch was obvious: home delivery offered the prospect of quality, reliability, freshness and, above all, convenience. Perishable baked goods should have fit right into the business model, yet bakeries faced a hurdle that dairy mavens did not. Culturally, middle-class white women were expected to demonstrate care for their family through the food they prepared, and breads and pies were among the most powerful symbols of a woman's role. If it was not a moral failing to refuse to bake, buying store-bought surely was.

Yet when cultural ideals meet lived realities, the results are often not clear cut, and out of necessity or preference, many women chose to challenge the conventions that confined them to the kitchen. The arrival of electric appliances and the increase in prepared and frozen foods accelerated changes that had begun a generation or two earlier, and women in the Jazz Age in particular, middle-class and otherwise, created new meanings for themselves. The jazz-hopped 1920s were a watershed in both culinary and women's history, introducing a new ethos of efficiency, and while the promised liberation from drudgery never fully materialized, home delivery of baked goods was a small step to leisure that women increasingly chose.

After the Civil War, several commercial bakers saw opportunity in delivering pies directly to customers. The New Yorker William Thompson rode his wagons to legendary status as a rags-to-riches story. Distressed by the low-quality pies he encountered everywhere, according to the legend, Thompson decided to do better himself, coming up with the idea of selling

Postcard from Huntt's Lunch Bakery, Lynn, Massachusetts, circa 1920. A typical New England bakery from the early twentieth century. *Collection of the author.*

Cooling racks with pies fresh from the oven, Granny's Pie Factory, East Hartford, Connecticut. *Photo by I. Eliot Wentworth, 2015.*

wholesale to restaurants and hotels, as his obituary claimed, "just as milk and other commodities were delivered." The trade became so lucrative that he was said to have earned more than $1 million on pies, which was some crust in those days.

Other urban pie entrepreneurs joined in the delivery game, selling their wares to caterers, restaurants, saloons or anyone who could not or would not cook. It was not that these companies delivered anything their customers could not prepare themselves. It is just that they provided predictable quality sweetened by convenience. In short order, the foot-bound pie man of folk song gave way to fleets of horse-drawn wagons and, eventually, to fleets of shiny trucks that connected cities and suburbs seamlessly. These could be small operations or industrial-scale. Mrs. Hopkins's Pies, another New York firm, was a recognizable brand from the late 1860s to at least the 1930s and was singled out in *Valentines Manual* as the first to fit out pie delivery vans "with rows of shelves on each side in cabinets" and the company name painted boldly on the side. In 1883, the *Washington Post* described the pie delivery phenomenon:

> *Pie-baking is a specialty, in which there are a number of persons engaged. Mrs. Hopkins commenced pie-baking very modestly in her own kitchen, and the brand became popular and is now trademark. Regular covered wagons, carrying each side stands with small shelves each holding one tin plate containing a pie, distribute pies by the gross to the trade; for pies are sold in lager beer saloons, drinking shops, restaurants, street booths, in fact, anywhere there is a chance for a demand for them…these pies are never made of fresh fruit or canned fruits but of preserved fruit…. Using preserved fruits the "line" of pies is the same the year through, and comprise all the fruits excepting the pineapple, and all the vegetables, such as pumpkin and rhubarb, but never squash or sweet potatoes, which are left to the resources of the housewives.*

In New England, a pair of pie purveyors—Cushman's Bakery and Table Talk Pies—blazed a regional trail in delivering baked goods in this new age of leisure. Nathan A. Cushman was a man who could only have been a baker. The son of Sylvester Cushman of Wilmington, Vermont, Nathan was one of seven sons in a single generation (and two sons-in-law) to enter the trade. His uncle, Horatio B. Cushman, had opened the first Cushman's Bakery in New York City in 1854, and after he asked Sylvester to join him as a partner after the Civil War, the extended family created an octopus of an empire of bakehouses, retail stores and spin-off enterprises that were icons in the city for nearly a century.

Like any ambitious princeling, Nathan felt the need for his own principality, and in 1908, he struck out for the floury pastures of Portland, Maine, bringing with him a big-city knowledge of high-volume baking. When Cushman's Bakery opened in January 1915, it represented itself as a paragon of progress and modernity, using only the purest ingredients and most efficient processes, while boasting of its ability to pump out an astonishing 1,800 loaves of bread per hour. Even on this scale, Cushman's plan was to sell direct to customers, delivering breads, cakes and pies through its horse-drawn fleet.

Despite his preparations, Cushman's wagons struggled out of the gate. As knowledgeable as he was about New York tastes, Cushman had to adapt to Maine, and even more, he had to adapt to a market caught in the throes of adjusting to what women would accept. He was fortunate. As women increasingly opted for convenience in the 1920s, Cushman's plan caught hold, and the company turned profitable. Pies flew out of plants and into homes in vast numbers, and during the shortages of the Second World War, the company's fortunes soared, enabling Cushman to expand into a second operation in Lynn, Massachusetts, and to replace its equine wagons with gasoline trucks, opening an opportunity for wider-ranging routes. At its peak, Cushman's was one of the largest retail bakeries in New England, but the postwar boom was surprisingly short-lived. The changes that lit a fire under their profits began to set fire to them. From frozen convenience foods to the rise of well-stocked suburban supermarkets, home delivery faded quickly, breaking the back of the Cushman scheme. Nathan Cushman contemplated continuing as a wholesaler, but in 1962, he sold out instead. The Lynn plant limped on until it, too, was sold in 1967, and the Portland operation whimpered into bankruptcy two years later.

Down in Massachusetts, Worcester had been an industrial hothouse for nearly a century and a magnet for European immigrants for nearly as long. Pulses of Irish, Italian, French, Poles, Lithuanians and other immigrants flocked in to work on the canals, railroads and mills. As Cushman's were

Opposite, top: Filling the pies, Table Talk factory, Worcester. *Photo by Leslie Jones, 1947. Print Department, Boston Public Library.*

Opposite, bottom: Covering pies before the trip to the oven, Table Talk factory, Worcester. *Photo by Leslie Jones, 1947. Print Department, Boston Public Library.*

Andy Koskinas guiding pies onto conveyor belt to furnace, Table Talk factory, Worcester. *Photo by Leslie Jones, 1947. Print Department, Boston Public Library.*

firing high in Portland, Theodore Tonna entered the scene. Tonna was born in the town of Bitola, Macedonia, where Greece and Albania crept together. According to family lore, Tonna was just twelve when his father was murdered by sheep rustlers, forcing him into exile to earn bread for his family. Trying his luck first in Pawtucket, Rhode Island, he eventually settled in Worcester in 1917 and, seven years later, entered into a partnership with a Greek immigrant, Angelus Cotsidas, and a friend Wilfred A. Casavant to form Table Talk Pies. The experiences of Tonna's young life had left him conversant in Greek, Italian, Albanian, Serbian and English, which neatly reflected what his workplace would become (and still is): a polyglot nursery for immigrants to enter American society. What better way to become American than making the all-American cherry pie?

Although the company flipped Cushman's business model on its head, Table Talk was no less successful at predicting women's changing attitudes toward the kitchen and other cultural trends. Rather than deliver pies to homes, in its early years the company specialized in

Table Talk four-inch cherry pie with tin pie plate. *Photo by I. Eliot Wentworth, 2015.*

supplying hotels and restaurants. By the 1930s, it had shifted into the retail trade, selling direct to customers through a retail shop on Green Street and, more importantly, selling to grocery stores and supermarkets. Its delivery network was as efficient and extensive as Cushman's, but it connected a different world. A neat convergence fueled the business: while women increasingly opted for convenience at home, restaurants increasingly opted for "homemade" on their menus. Table Talk, the industrial master, was home. For years, Table Talk pies were sold in tin plates (like Connecticut's famous Frisbie pies) for which customers left a deposit, almost guaranteeing return business. Early on, their plates were emblazoned with the motto "Mother's only rival."

Like Cushman's, Table Talk could be relied on for excellent ingredients, using only wild blueberries, for instance, instead of cultivated, and its quality control was famous. For an outfit founded by immigrants and staffed largely by immigrants, they were keenly aware of New Englanders' tastes. Apple was consistently the most popular pie, but cherry waxed annually on Washington's birthday, pumpkin carved its niche at Thanksgiving (when the plant now moves to a 24/7 operation) and custard pies were inexplicably more popular around Easter. Ten thousand Boston cream pies per week were more than enough. By the early 1950s, Table Talk was delivering 1 million pies per week all around the Northeast, more than any bakery in the region, and employing 250 bakers on a staff of 800.

Like Cushman's, Table Talk found need for a new direction by the 1960s, facing the perpetual challenges of changing consumer preferences. Rather than fight, Tonna and partners seized an offer in 1965 to sell out to Beech-Nut for an estimated $15 million to $20 million. The firm was less fortunate. Without the vision of its founders, the company declined in the 1970s, ceasing operations entirely in 1984. To the relief of pie lovers, the family intervened, and Tonna's son Christo Cocaine purchased the company back in 1986, returning it to profitability.

The key to this turnaround was the company's ability to recognize the next step in America's culture of convenience, as well as its willingness to adapt. Making the strategic decision to focus on the inexpensive end of the snack market, its four-inch pies have become fixtures in New England supermarkets such as Market Basket, Stop and Shop or Big Y, and on the side, it bakes pies for private labels, including Entenmann's. As profits rose, Table Talk turned its attention back to larger sizes, and it now makes frozen pies as well for sale nationally.

Flaunting its status as champion of the cheap, Table Talk pies are shockingly good. While not exactly a taste safari, they are not exactly an afternoon in the chemistry lab either, eschewing the preservatives and artificial ingredients that pump up their competitors. But the important thing is taste. Avoiding the mortal sin of many snack pies, over-sweetness, while also ignoring the virtues of the sharp bite that cherries can deliver, the pie is an exercise in moderation. As much as anything, it is distinguished by its crust, which manages to be simultaneously light and prominent and delightfully free of the glazes that ruin so many mass-market pastries. The four-inch pie announces itself by the crisp rim where top and bottom crusts meet, giving taste and texture that travels well. It is a small indulgence and cheap, but an indulgence nonetheless.

According to the *Oxford Companion to American Food and Drink*, cherry pie dropped in popularity beginning in the 1870s as early nutritionists and home economists began to define what a healthy diet should be. As beloved as the pie was, it had been a target of abuse by health advocates for years. As early as the 1840s, the starchy vegetarian William Alcott, whose sleep was disturbed by all manner of cooked food, warned about the choking hazard of cherry pits, ending his rant:

> *A meal of cherries, whether it be breakfast or dinner, should always be moderate in quantity, and slowly swallowed; and as I have before insisted,*

the stones should be rejected, as much as if they were poisonous. All cooking of cherries is inadmissible, and for many and various reasons. The cherry puddings and pies of our country, are much prized by many; but they are a most stupid concern, to say nothing of their tendency on health.

In fact, pie was condemned, roundly. Sarah Tyson Rorer, the most prominent of a new generation of health reformers at the turn of the century, singled out pies for opprobrium, slamming them in her column in the culinary magazine *Table Talk* (yes, *Table Talk*) and in articles titled "Why I Have No Cakes and Pies on My Table" (1905) and "Why I Oppose Pies" (1900). "The inside of a pie is injurious," she complained, insisting that "pies and cakes are indigestible."

But the purity of the cherry and its simple surface survived such assaults—no healthier, but no less worse for the wear. Made at home, delivered or picked up at a convenience store, they follow their makers and endure.

RECIPES

Tart of Cherries (Salmon, 1710)

Stone your Cherries, and lay them in the bottom of your Pye, with beaten Cinamon, Ginger, and Sugar, then close it up, bake it and ice it, when it is baked, pour into it Muskadine and D.R.W. [Damask Rose Water] well mingled together, and scrape on Sugar.

Ripe Fruit Pies (Beecher, 1850)

Peach, Cherry, Plum, Currant, and Strawberry.—Line your dish with paste. After picking over and washing the fruit carefully (peaches must be pared, and the rest picked from the stem), place a layer of fruit and a layer of sugar in your dish, until it is well filled, then cover it with paste, and trim the edge neatly, and prick the cover. Fruit pies require about an hour to bake in a thoroughly heated oven.

Berry Pies (Parloa, 1880)

Line the plates, and fill as full as you can with berries, and dredge on about half a spoonful of flour, and two spoonfuls of sugar, and two of water; cover as directed for sliced apple pies, and bake forty minutes in a moderate oven. All berry pies are made in this manner, if they are very sour using more sugar. Cherries and currants do not require any water, but more sugar, and they must not be heaped in the plate as blueberries, blackberries, raspberries, and strawberries are.

Whortleberry Pie (Howland, 1845)

Make common paste; line a deep plate with it, put in your berries, cover them over thick with sugar; a little butter sliced on adds to the flavor; cover it over with the crust, and bake it an hour.

Very good pies may be made in the same way of cherries, blackberries, or raspberries.

AUGUST

A RADICAL PROPOSITION

Near the imaginary line where New Hampshire and Massachusetts meet, old pastures have mostly grown into deep woods, although clearings here and there make openings where back-to-landers could find cheap farmland in the 1960s and 1970s. These woods once teemed with young men and women—urbanites mostly, utopians all—who hoped to find peace and meaningful connection in places like Total Loss Farm, Red Clover, the Sirius Community, Earthlands or the Brotherhood of the Spirit, places guided by politics or spirit or desire for an alternative. It was always the quest. Their numbers have lessened through time, but here and there are openings where their legacy lives.

I was visiting friends in this liminal land, poised between pasts and presents, two old radicals whose paths had converged in the Liberation News Service and never quite parted since. Allen had left New Left activism for these woods in 1973 and helped found a pioneering gay men's commune (an activist act if there ever was one), and Katya was the pioneering feminist who had roved the nation from New York to Oregon and Florida through careers in journalism, education and healthcare. They are remarkable people, writers and thinkers and fans of the pie.

That morning, Allen and Katya picked berries on the slopes behind the house and decided on pie. Blueberries were in high season, and both agreed they should star. But when it came to raspberries, still bustling, the concord evaporated. Katya's suggestion that the fruits played well together in a "very berry" pie raised an eyebrow across the kitchen and

Slicing the very berry pie. *Photo by I. Eliot Wentworth, 2014.*

a dubious shake of Allen's head. When it comes to pie, at least this day, he was a purist.

Katya won the debate and assembled a top "crust" of granola, flake cereal (Special K), honey, butter and cinnamon, a perfect complement for a delicate filling. When cooled and sliced (skin warm), the wedges surrendered gracefully to the law of gravity without the expected deluge. This pie is all about the fruit, picked at its morning peak, warmed in the sun at midday and baked by the afternoon. Sugar is nothing more than a murmur in the throat, and the savory crust is mere contrast. A person comes to this pie for fruit, the whole fruit and nothing but the fruit—or is it *fruits?*

New England summers are a riot of berries. Berries on berries. We were favored and flavored with oceans of small ripe fruits, according to Henry David Thoreau, our radical sage of the backwoods. "We do not realize how rich our country is in berries," he wrote. He rejoiced in them. When it came to the noble whortleberry, the English mustered only two varieties to fourteen in America, and fully eleven of ours were edible. Wherever one looked, there they were. "One kind or another flourishes in every soil and locality," Thoreau boasted. "The Pennsylvania and Canada blueberries especially in elevated, cool, and airy places, on hills and mountains, in openings in the woods and in sproutlands." Ours was a country stained in dark blue.

Long before the colonial invasion, whortleberries were favorites of New England's native inhabitants, whether eaten fresh or dried for the winter, and the colonists took these preferences for their own. Blueberries and the American cranberry—both members of the extraordinary genus *Vaccinium*—are the only two fruits native to North America to become commercially cultivated, although it took years for each to get there. No one took the trouble to cultivate cranberries until about 1800, and the blueberry was ignored until the 1920s. There was just no need: they were free for all who wished to gather them and grew so abundantly on lands that would otherwise lie waste that they were cheaper to gather than to tend.

In Thoreau's time, the term "whortleberry" could refer to almost any round, blue-tinged *Vaccinium*, but botanically, whortleberry, hurtleberry, huckleberry, bilberry and blueberry represented a wide range of distinct fruits. Lest we forget, there are also distinctions between high-bush, low-bush and half-high hybrids of blueberries alone, but let us keep our eyes on the pies. Wilson Flagg, a friend of Thoreau's and the "apostle of the trees," wrote half-jokingly that whortleberries referred to fruits we gathered, while huckleberries were what we sold. He parsed the confounding genus carefully, explaining that when it came to culinary use, the whortleberry was "less acidulous, less mucilaginous" and bore a harder seed than the blueberry. No, they were not identical, and however often they conflated them, Americans eventually caught on. Gradually beginning in the 1860s, inexorably, New Englanders' linguistic preferences shifted from the whortleberry to the sweet and gentle blueberry, and in cookbooks, one term effectively replaced the other.

No one esteemed this "peculiarly American fruit" more than Flagg. Not even the cherry held such a high position in the hierarchy of New England fruits, he claimed, and if we were to suffer the extinction of one, it would be the whortleberry we rued. "Millions of bushels" were gathered during a long harvest season that stretched from July through September, and the whortleberry outstripped even the cranberry as "one of our staple productions." For impoverished New Englanders especially, the berry boom meant monetary boon, providing a way for even the smallest children to contribute to the larder and pocketbook alike. It was not just taste or even lavish lucre that elevated the whortleberry for New Englanders: whortleberrying excursions became beloved social events, bringing a communal sense to lands where communes would later thrive, and they were virtually rites of passage. In July 1853, the pseudonymous "Amenia" recalled her whortleberrying "frolics" for the inquisitive *New York Times*:

Nothing can be more amusing than one of these loads [of whortleberry pickers]; *the old lumber wagon, drawn by the laziest and gentlest nags; the broken straw hats, and the faded sun-bonnets, half-hiding laughing faces and roguish eyes; the mock gravity of the old, and the sportive gaiety of the young; some holding big baskets in their laps, and some tin pails; some whipping the horses with a hazel branch, and others tickling the girls' necks with a straw; some wondering when the mountain will be reached, and others singing "Rosa Lee" with the gleefulness of black-birds. Then what times we used to have climbing mountains, and breaking a path through the bushes. Betty would tear her frock, and New would lose his hat down the rocks. One of the men would probably kill a rattlesnake, and another a rabbit. Finally, in some open space where the trees had been cut for a couple of years, we would find the berries…*

Testing the waters of their independence, young boys and girls dove into the woods and swamps on the hunt for berries, and if the newspapers of the day were to be believed, they did so at their own peril, separated as they were from the protection of family and friends. There was the notorious case of Mary Stannard, lured to a patch of berries in Madison, Connecticut, and murdered by Reverend Herbert Hayden, and newspapers never hesitated to report on violent assaults, kidnappings, rapes and run-ins with deadly animals whenever women or children left civilization for the wild woods. In the late summer of 1880 alone, the *New York Times* reported the grisly discovery of the corpse of a female hermit who had died while gathering whortleberries, and less than a month later, the paper moved on to discuss a pair of whortleberrying boys who waged a "hard fight" with rattlesnakes, killing thirty-eight with nothing but rocks and sticks—and lots of testosterone. Snakes always get a bad rap, but the dangers were intrinsic to becoming an adult and part of how whortleberries entered the conscience of so many New Englanders.

Long considered a regional specialty of New Hampshire and Maine, whortleberry pie resembled cherry pie in that neither earned as much ink in cookbooks as their reputation would suggest. As was the case with cherries, early Americans preferred whortleberry pies in their purest state, often nothing more than sugar and berries in a crust, leaving fruit to state its own case. Allen would be proud. In 1830, the frugal Lydia Maria Child wrote that whortleberries made "a very good common pie, where there is a large family of children," presumably because the children could be silenced by sending them into the woods for the fruit, but she added the unusual touch of a little ground clove.

Blueberry pie, as distinct from whortleberry, has more cryptic beginnings, but it was just as pure. The first use of the name "blueberry pie" may be a passing reference in the *New England Farmer* for November 1829, describing a visit to an obstreperous New England inn keeper, but the pie is surely older. Actual recipes for blueberry pie, per se, may have awaited Mrs. Bliss's *Practical Cook Book* in 1850, with its instructions to vent the pie by cutting a slit in the top crust before baking. Bliss was on to something that has troubled blueberry piemakers before and since. How does one keep a soft fruit pie from becoming a tsunami of gush? This was more than a theoretical debate between Katya and Allen; it was a long-simmering concern that kept many a bad poet up at night, as noted in the *Boston Globe* on August 7, 1905:

> *I dearly love blueberry pie,*
> *But it does not agree with me.*
> *All afternoon I squirm and sigh,*
> *And then at night strange things I see.*
> *Temptation comes, I say once more:*
> *"I wonder if 'twill hurt me now,*
> *As it has always done before."*
>
> *And then I always give myself*
> *The benefit of all the doubt,*
> *And eat the flaky, fragrant pie,*
> *With purplish juice all running out.*
> *"I wonder if 'twill hurt me now,"*
> *I say again, and then—Ah me!*
> *All afternoon I squirm and sigh,*
> *And all the night strange things I see.*

Controlling the "purplish juice" while retaining a crisp finish to the crust was quite a task for lovers of the fruit pie. Bliss's slit top might vent the steam and lower the moisture, and playful pie-birds might sing their part while looking good, but neither was fully reliable for stanching the berry's flow. Sarah Josepha Hale recommended inverting a teacup under the crust to collect the juice as the pie cooked, which had the virtue of greater capacity, and more adventurous bakers wove their top crust into a lattice, but neither the beauty of the results nor the appealing surfeit of crispy edges were protection against the billowing waves of a fluid fruit.

Stepping up the game, cooks turned to ebbing the purple tide by employing thickeners. In the mid-1840s, Mrs. Cornelius recommending dredging berries in flour, and cornstarch came along later as a substitute, but in the hands of amateurs both can result in a cloudy or gummy interior. The real Yankee innovation may be tapioca. By the 1890s, tapioca had been known for more than a century as a bland and starchy source of nutrition for the sick. Patients who could hold nothing else down were thought to be able to handle this derivative of cassava. During the yellow fever epidemics of the 1790s, physicians Benjamin Rush and Richard Bayley recommended it—along with sago, salep and panado (boiled bread)—for victims, and in 1795, Peter Anderson thought it could stand in as mother's milk for a needy child.

Attached as it was to the diets of the sick and invalid, tapioca caught on slowly as a dessert. Catherine Beecher and Mrs. Lincoln did their best by promoting puddings, although Beecher calling it "healthful and unstimulating" might not have helped. As late as 1904, Fannie Farmer still considered tapioca to be wallpaper for the stomach, with just enough calories and nutrients to encourage any invalid to seek better food. Minute Tapioca and modern nutrition helped to change things by introducing the convenience of quick cooking, using a process invented by Susan Stavers in 1883. A struggling landlady from Boston, Stavers discovered that grinding cassava fine produced reliably smooth puddings and quick cook times. The recipe was sold to John Whitman in 1894, and production was moved to the western Massachusetts town of Orange, where Minute Tapioca salvaged the region's fruit pies by absorbing liquids, retaining flavors and keeping the texture this side of gelatin. Not everyone likes the sometimes gummy results (Katya does not), but the brand remains popular.

Blueberry pies have gone on to become picnic stars and teeth-staining terrors. In urban bakeries like the remarkable Kay's Pastry Shop in Holyoke, Massachusetts, the blueberry is always a best seller. Kay's (like the astonishing Donut Dip a few miles away) seems to have dozed since the 1950s in appearance and price, but the pies are fresh and heavier than it seems possible due to the depth of fruit and heft of crust. The customers all seem to be regulars, the people behind the counter equally so, and on either side, Kay's people do not mince words (maybe pies) in ordering donuts, pies and whatever else they have in production that day. The blueberry pie has the character of much-loved pies of the past, too, the kind that Nicola Sacco was reported by the *Boston Globe* to have requested before he and his fellow anarchist Bartolomeo Vanzetti were executed for a bomb they did not plant. Kay's serves the old kind of pie that has suffered only the occasional indignity

Kays Bakery, Holyoke, Massachusetts, during temporary closure—the archetype of an urban bakery. *Photo by I. Eliot Wentworth, 2015.*

since, like the fad for meringue toppings in 1920s. It is a pie has remained a radical proposition in keeping with backwoods pie made by Katya and Allen—that the purity of a perfect fruit will prevail.

I will side with Allen on this one. Living simply has its own rewards.

RECIPES

Whortleberry Pie (Howland, 1845)

Make common paste; line a deep plate with it, put in your berries, cover them over thick with sugar; a little butter sliced on adds to the flavor; cover it over with the crust, and bake it an hour. Very good pies may be made in the same way of cherries, blackberries, or raspberries.

Blueberry Pie (Bliss, 1850)

Wash the blueberries in a colander, with cold water, and let them drain a few minutes; then pour them into a deep dish (a soup plate) lined with Paste No. 8, cover them with four table-spoonfuls of fine white sugar, dredge them with flour, cover them with the same paste, wet and pinch together the edges of the pastes, cut a slit in the centre of the top crust, through which the steam may escape, and bake in a quick oven forty-five minutes.

Blueberry Pie (Farmer, 1896)

2 ½ cups berries
flour
½ cup sugar
⅛ teaspoon salt

Line a deep plate with Plain Paste, fill with berries slightly dredged with flour; sprinkle with sugar and salt, cover, and bake forty-five to fifty minutes in a moderate oven. For sweetening, some prefer to use one-third molasses, the remaining two-thirds to be sugar. Six green grapes (from which seeds have been removed) cut in small pieces much improve the flavor, particularly where huckleberries are used in place of blueberries.

Blueberry Pie (Democratic Women of Maine, circa 1929)

A medium-sized rather deep pie plate is needed for thick, juicy pies. Sift a tablespoon flour over the bottom of the dough-lined plate, put in a scant quart of berries, about one-half cup sugar (the first berries require more), butter half size nutmeg, and another tablespoon flour over the berries before putting on the top crust. Bake in moderate oven.

SEPTEMBER

MOCKING THE BERRY

Before industrialization, before urbanization and electrification, before canals and railroads, airplanes and the internal combustion engine hemmed in the miles, New Englanders ate local. It wasn't so much that they led isolated lives, although sometimes it may have felt that way, or that they lived on the edge of the world. Indeed, every spring, crowds of young New Englanders, rich and poor, rushed the ports to light out for Ishmael years at sea, wandering deep highways off the coasts of South America, Africa and Asia. In the homes of the elite, with their global connections through commerce and kin, Caribbean sugar and exotic fruits were served on Chinese platters and laid out in parlors lit by Pacific whale oil. But these connections had less impact on the rule of diet: food was experienced through the pulse of abundance and absence, a seasonal pulse of fruits and berries, vegetables and grains. To imagine food was to imagine season—to imagine the fresh profusion of harvest set against the months of salted, dried, pickled and preserved. Fruits, in particular, defined the calendar's warmest pages. Rhubarb signified the break of May, followed by strawberries in June and a steady thrum of cherries, gooseberries, raspberries and blueberries, peaches, pears and apples.

Of all the fruits that pulsed through the New England larder, the cranberry had perhaps the strongest beat. If cherries were a quaver in the heat and whortleberries a slow dirge, the cranberry was an opera. A North American native, the tart red awakening was a favorite of the early colonists, and it fueled an lively international trade based solely on the vines that straggled wild across the region's waste lands. With nothing more than a pail and a pair of hands, the poor could earn critical support for winter by harvesting and selling wild fruit, at least until horticulturists tamed the cranberry and shifted the balance from workers to owners.

After its first successful cultivation around the War of 1812, the cranberry was rapidly developed into a major industry of manicured bogs and far-flung merchants that beat to a rhythm of its own. From winter through summer, the bogs waxed small and smaller, requiring only a handful of workers to maintain, but harvest time was another affair. During an intense burst of six to eight weeks, growers required so many pickers, talliers, sorters and haulers that they rapidly outstripped the local labor supply as the industry grew, and all the innovations in equipment and operational efficiency barely helped.

To meet the demand for labor, a united nations of immigrants rode to the rescue. Already skilled at surviving the seasonal uncertainties that afflicted the working classes, gangs of Finns, "Kanakas" (Polynesians), Irish, Italians, Azoreans and Cape Verdeans fled the quarries, mills and piers in early September to descend onto the bogs to pick the Early Black berries as they matured to sweet and delicate perfection, after which they crawled their way, variety by variety, across the sand and peat to bring in the Dennis, McFarlin and Mathews until late in October; the Howes also arrived with its tart taste and exceptional shelf life.

The natural cycle of the cranberry made it the perfect fruit for the long fall. Its hallowed place as an anchor of the Thanksgiving table is no mere coincidence. But until canning and juicing became common in the early twentieth century, the cranberry virtually disappeared from the table once the holidays were over. Until freezers and modern preservatives became available, berry fans had to deal with two related problems: what to do with the exuberant excess when fruit was available and what to do in the rest of the year when it wasn't. The cranberry had one thing going for it: it stored better than most other fruits, giving options for those who wished to make the most of its abundance. Cranberry lovers discovered early on that berries, bottled dry and sealed, could last for months, and as early as 1847, one of the fruit's great boosters, David Choate, lamented that cooks too often ignored cranberries in favor of less palatable alternatives:

> *Most families are compelled to rely for half the year upon apples for sauce and pies; and the pickled cucumber, indigestible and dangerous as it is, and often thrown away, as it always ought to be, is retained upon the farmer's table, merely because it is the only thing of the kind known that can be kept through the year…. What an opportunity to bring forward and substitute the pure acid of the cranberry! For culinary purposes, it must be cheaper. Apples are held to be unfit for pie or sauce, till every element of the natural flavor almost is*

destroyed or neutralized by the rose-water and the spice. But give to cranberries the quantum sufficit of one single thing, "sweet cane," and they never tire.

Although beloved in early America for its "pure acid" kick, the cranberry was less noted for its versatility. Here and there one finds recipes for an odd pudding or dumpling, and the abolitionist, feminist and culinary expert Lydia Maria Child found that half a raw berry laid cut-side down could remove corns from the feet, but the inevitable fate of nearly every cranberry was to merge with a helping of "sweet cane" in filling sauce pans, jelly jars or pie crusts. Even within a pie crust, there wasn't much adventure. Writers like Child or Mrs. Cornelius admitted that cranberry pies and tarts could succeed with or without an upper crust, but their recipes for the filling seldom varied beyond small adjustments in the proportion of berries to sugar (ranging by taste from 1:1 to 2:1) or in the inclusion of a splash of lemon or dash of cinnamon, nutmeg or mace. Even with these additions, cooks seldom strayed far. "Cranberry pies," Child noted, "need very little spice." So simple in concept were cranberry pies that few cookbook writers felt it necessary to say more than Fannie Farmer, whose terse instructions were to "put ingredients in saucepan in order given," cook for ten minutes, "cool, and bake in one crust, with a rim, and strips across the top."

As the cranberry industry grew in the years after the Civil War and the taste for the berries grew with it, New Englanders reluctantly abandoned their hidebound ways and began to experiment with new ways of using the tart stuff. When the quiet revolution hit Waterville, Maine, for example, Mrs. G.P. Colby responded by adding eggs into the filling of a classic cranberry pie and topping it with a sweet meringue, and more notably, three of her fellow Watervilleans set the tone for a trend to come: making cranberries seem less like cranberries. In answer to the question of how cooks dealt with the waxing and waning pulse of fruits, these three women replied in a quintessentially American way: if you can't beat the berry, mock it. It is to them and women like them that we owe the short-lived fad for the mock cherry pie.

For many of us of a particular generation, the mere mention of culinary mockery evokes a shuddering recollection of the mock apple pie, that unspeakable novelty of the Eisenhower era. For many, this sacrilegious mockery seems nothing more than a plot by corporate crackers to foist processed foods on an unsuspecting public by disguising them as old favorites. We may not be far off, but it is worth noting that in English or American cooking, mockery is nothing new, and the reasons for it are as varied as the cooks who mock. While some cooks looked only to substitute cheaper ingredients for more expensive, others come to mock foods that are taboo, unhealthy or disapproved, while others still hope only to cover up for scarcity due to season, location or rationing. Mockery can also be a fine way of demonstrating culinary versatility, creativity and skill; some cooks, in the end, mock in hopes of conjuring new magic from ingredients that seem all too common.

The vogue for turtle flesh that accompanied the rise of the British empire, for example, led to high prices for the marine reptile that, in turn, produced a vogue for the inexpensive sham, mock turtle soup. This famous fraud for an infamous dish was included in one of the earliest cookbooks published in the United States, Susannah Carter's *Frugal Housewife* (1772), and it found its way into Hannah Glasse's *Art of Cookery*, ubiquitous in early American homes. From the start, then, mockery was as American as apple pie. Not content with mocking reptiles alone, we see that Glasse offered to mock hare and oyster sauce, while in 1792, Francis Collingwood mocked ginger, which he attempted to imitate by using cauliflower steeped in wine vinegar, spices, garlic, horseradish, cayenne pepper and turmeric. Anything could be mocked. Even as improvements in trade and transport increased the availability of foodstuffs in the early nineteenth century, the mockery was unrelenting. As bold as anyone, William Kitchiner's mockery (1830) extended to hare, goose, mutton broth, pheasant and venison, and lest the vegetable kingdom felt deprived, he mocked sauces of gooseberry (made of rhubarb), tomatoes and capers. Kitchiner was pleased with his deception: his mock turtle soup, he wrote, "was eaten by the committee of taste with unanimous applause, and they pronounced it a very satisfactory substitute for the 'far-fetch'd and dear-bought' turtle; which is entirely indebted for its title of 'sovereign of savouriness,' to the rich soup with which it is surrounded."

For their own reasons, vegetarians have been nearly as inventive in mockery as Kitchiner. The Theosophists of Los Angeles mocked steak, creamed chicken and pot roast, while the House of David (1956) mocked turkey, salmon, crab, chicken croquettes and even chop suey, which much have set some kind of record as a mockery of mockery. If imitation is the sincerest form of flattery, mock foods are a sincere indication of foods most desired.

But why mock pies, humble as they are? Whatever the reasons, cooks have been mocking pies for generations. In fact, that most renowned mockery of all, the mock apple pie, is not the spawn of Eisenhower at all but rather the proud descendant of the "chemical apple pie," an early nineteenth-century concoction slapped between prebaked crusts that included crushed crackers, sugar and cream of tartar and nary a whiff of fruit. Our consumerist relic was also the cousin of the austere "cracker pie" that Confederate women baked during the ordeal of the Civil War. "To one small bowl of crackers that have been soaked until no hard parts remain," they recommended, "add one teaspoonful of tartaric acid, sweeten to your taste, add some butter, and a very little nutmeg." In theory, the cream of tartar tricked the taste buds, providing just enough acidic kick that the unholy mixture passed muster as authentic fruit. Until one thought about it. Or tasted it.

Beyond apples, there was a whole world of pie mockery. Reading the lines between its exhortations to support foreign missions, *The Wayside Gleanings* cookbook (1889) from Athol, Massachusetts, carried recipes for mock lady cake, mock loaf cake and a "mock meat pie," in which rolled crackers joined eggs, sugar, molasses, butter, vinegar, raisins, clove, cinnamon and nutmeg to make a completely unconvincing beef. The Ladies Aid Society of the Baptist Church in Norwich, Massachusetts (1907), doubled up with its twin recipes for mock mince meat, while the Unitarians of Waterville, Maine (1898), mysteriously mocked the innocent pumpkin with sweet potato:

> *Line deep pie tins with good rich crust. Mash and measure two cups of cooked sweet potato. Beat with it two eggs, one cup sugar, three cups of milk, a teaspoonful each of ginger and cinnamon. Fill the crusts and bake slowly one hour. These are better than most pumpkin pies.*

The mockery kept rolling: New Englanders' fondness for pies triggered a mock cream pie from the Baptists of Wallingford, Vermont (1907), and a mock lemon pie from the Resolute Grange in Brownville, Maine (1913), in which rhubarb and sugar stood in for the bitter fruit. With the First World War, mockery reached its peak. With a food crisis threatening the nation, Helen Watkeys Moore responded with her patriotic *Camouflage Cookery*, an entire book of mock dishes that sported "palatable and economical recipes" for Americans who wished "to prepare wholesome and appetizing" meals that bore no resemblance to reality. An expert in culinary responses to social crises, Moore went on the next year to publish the gem *On Uncle Sam's Water Wagon*, a cookbook celebrating the Constitutional amendment that brought Prohibition to the land.

Patriotism, scarcity, crisis and cost were powerful incentives, but cranberries came into the mock equation mostly due to their sheer profusion. That fall-time burst of berries and the brief window in which they could be used forced cooks to choose between being repetitive or being creative. Creativity won out, even in stodgy New England. Somewhere up here, an unnamed cook of the Gilded Age looked at the roundness of the cranberry and the roundness of the cherry and decided that she could swap one for the other. The mock cherry pie was born.

Cherries, of course, made prized pies, but they were highly perishable, barely outlasting their brief season, leaving pie-lovers longing for months on end. The mock cherry pie was a clever way of satisfying that longing and an even cleverer way of shoveling more and more of the profligate cranberries down the gullets of New England families. After the *Chicago Record Cook Book* carried a recipe in 1896, the dish proliferated wildly. The fraud was perpetrated by employing an odd quartet of cranberries, raisins, sugar and vanilla, almost always assembled as described in the poetical words of the *Cambridge Cookbook* of 1909:

If you've ne'er eat mock cherry pie
Here's a receipt I wish you'd try:
Two cups of cranberries you will need;
One cup of raisins free from seed;
One cup of sugar, more or less;
Now put in tray and chop the mess.
Add two-thirds cup of water cold,
One tablespoon of flour to hold;
Vanilla, added to your taste;
And all inclose in nice rich paste.
Now ope your mouth and close your eye,—
You'll think you're eating cherry pie.
—Mrs. Nellie Mason Hodges

Whether mock cherry pie actually tastes like cherries (not much to me), it spread quickly. Featuring the pie in its cooking demonstrations, the Boston Cooking School aided and abetted its renown, but the women of New England seized the pie for their own. The best gauge of popularity was the zeal with which everyday women submitted recipes for the pie to newspapers and the innumerable charitable cookbooks they produced as fundraisers for churches and social organizations. Often lovingly signed by contributors, these recipes were not always original creations, as sometimes assumed, but they were always demonstrations of a cook's commitment to a cause—whether to a church or social group—and were testimony to refined taste and domestic skill. These recipes were such favorites at home that women sought to share them publicly with friends and community, often signing their names to the recipe for posterity.

As early as 1898, the Unitarian women of Waterville, Maine, could hardly restrain themselves in extolling the virtues of mock cherry pie, offering three distinct versions in one cookbook, while the church women of Laconia, New Hampshire (1904), and Andover, Massachusetts (1913), each required four to have their say, despite including straight cranberry pie as well. Nor did the recipes differ all that much: beyond subtle variations in the ratio of cranberry to raisin to sugar (from 2:1:2 to equal parts all around), the pies are nearly identical. They were so beloved that repetition was necessary.

The taste for mock cherry pie declined after the Second World War, perhaps because cherries became more widely available year-round and perhaps because the cranberry industry developed other uses for their fruit. When a mock cherry pie appears, it appears as much as a quaint anachronism as a viable recipe for the modern age. As the quirks of the year have evened out and as we live less local lives, our mockery has moved to other realms of desire.

RECIPES

Cranberry Tart (Hale, 1852)

To every pint of cranberries, allow a teaspoonful of lemon-juice, and three ounces of good moist sugar. First, pour all the juice of your cranberries into a basin; then well wash the cranberries in a pan, with plenty of water, pick out all the bad ones, and put the cranberries into a dish; add to them the sugar and lemon-juice, pour the juice out of the basin gently to them, so as to leave behind the dirt and sediment which will settle at the bottom; mix all together, and let it lie while you are making your pie—thus: line the bottom of your dish with puff-paste not quite a quarter of an inch thick, put your cranberries upon it, without any juice, and cover with the same paste not quite half an inch thick; close the edges as usual, ice it, and bake it from three-quarters of an hour to an hour, according to size. Simmer the juice a few minutes, which serve up with your tart in a small sauce tureen. A pint of cranberries makes a pretty sized tart.

Cranberry Pie with Eggs
(Ladies of the Unitarian Church, Waterville, Maine, 1898)

Take one coffee cupful of finely chopped cranberries, and a cup of sugar, beaten with one egg, and the yolks of two eggs. Mix them thoroughly and turn into a plate lined with pie crust, and bake in a moderate oven. Beat the whites of two eggs to a stiff froth, and add two tablespoonfuls of sugar. When the pie is baked, spread the meringue roughly over the top and return to the oven for a few moments to brown lightly.—Mrs. G.P. Colby

Cranberry Pie (Orange Universalist Church Cookbook, 1928)

1 cup cranberries, chopped
⅔ cup sugar
2 tbsp. flour
½ cup raisins
1 cup hot water
1 tsp. vanilla

Bake in two crusts.—Mrs. Jennie Munsell

Mock Cherry Pie (Ladies First Baptist Church of Gloucester, 1899)

One cup of cranberries; cut into each with a knife (this will keep them from bursting and cooking to pieces); one cup of sugar, half a cup of water, one tablespoonful of flour, wet in a little of the water, a pinch of salt. Stir all together and bake between two crusts. Make an opening in the center of the upper crust.—Carol F. Pattillo.

Note: This same recipe can be found partly verbatim in the Chicago Record Cook Book of 1896 attributed to Mrs. Olive P. Abbott of Reading, Michigan, who added, "The pie should be baked early in the day, or before the roast is in the oven, as the steam and smoke will ruin pie crust."

Mock Cherry Pie (State of Maine Cook Book, circa 1929)

One cup cranberries, one-half cup raisins, one cup boiling water. Place over fire to cook a few minutes, add one cup sugar mixed with a tablespoon of flour, one teaspoon of vanilla. This makes a small pie. If a larger one is desired, take one and one-half cups of cranberries, three-fourths cup raisins, and a little more water. I prefer strips of pastry for the top crust.—Mrs. Fred. B. Edwards, Brooks (Maine)

OCTOBER

A Most Persistent Pie

Perched on a sloping street in Plymouth, Blue Blinds Bakery seemed like a fine place for a slice of apple pie on a rainy afternoon. It was October after all, apple season, and just a few weeks before the three hundred and umpteenth anniversary of the Pilgrims' first landing in the New World—although that would have been at Provincetown, not Plymouth. Still, it seemed strangely appropriate to be standing on the steps of a restaurant in that historic town, thinking of all that past and all that memory, looking down the street past the Mayflower House Museum to where a chip off Plymouth Rock still lies. It was like one myth wrapped inside another and then another: the myth of where the Puritan separatists landed wrapped inside the myth of American origins wrapped inside a pie that everyone from baseball teams to H. Rap Brown assures us is all-American. You don't need a telescope to see what apple pie means to the New England soul.

Inside, Blue Blinds has the feel of a neighbor's home, if that home had a bakery counter installed in the living room, and with a few coffee drinkers nattering away on their cellphones to serve as background music, it seemed a right place for pie adventure. Breaking from their own conversation, a gaggling pair of teenagers behind the counter announced that all their baked goods were made with organic and all-natural ingredients and then advised us that there were two pies on tap that afternoon—irrelevant for me given my apple fixation but a sore temptation for my friend. Both were delicious, they said—not did they oversell. Although the apple was a sweeter pie than I usually prefer, and a little reticent in the crust, the slice that arrived on our table was a wonderment: a tall pile of crisp fruit with a mysterious pink blush that made it seem shyer than its sharp edges. It must have been a cinnamon blush, but my mind went to rose water with the color.

Because this was Plymouth, it was hard not to think of history while wolfing down, even if the history is not straightforward. You see, Blue Blinds is no relic of Puritan days, no vestige of a colonial past or even a colonial revival; it dates only from the venerable year of 2008. But like an apple plucked from an historical tree, Blue Blinds polishes well in the light. This was not just any bakery; it was the public face of a quintessentially American religious community, the Twelve Tribes, a small slice of our common past.

From the time of the Puritans, America has been a veritable orchard of religious innovation, sowed in groups like the Twelve Tribes that are dedicated to restoring the "primitive church" but that yield fruit that is disconcertingly new. Founded in the early 1970s as a ministry to homeless youth in Tennessee, the Twelve Tribes seems at first glance like so many other spiritual experiments of that era, especially those of the holy children of the counterculture, the so-called Jesus Freaks. From the outset, the Twelve Tribes rejected Christian denominations (which rejected it right back), looking on organized churches as hopelessly corrupt, but at the same time, it rejected the excesses of its hippie peers. It sought something different. Instead of conforming to a church, it formed its own communities as a step toward a "tribal life." Living "collectively in households," members surrendered worldly possessions, pooled resources, lived simply and worked "together for the common good." Unlike many other communal groups, they did not reject free enterprise; they embraced it, collectively. The Community, as the Twelve Tribes is called, has become known to outsiders primarily through its "cottage industries" and especially for its string of natural food restaurants and bakeries that are supplied, in some cases, by produce from its own organic farms. Kosher Jews, halal Muslims and non-caffeinated Mormons all remind us of how deeply intertwined food and spirituality can be, and the spiritual tenets that have led the Community to embrace organic and "natural" foods are no less profound.

This uncanny mix of piety, communalism and business was too much for the 1970s south to digest, and facing the enmity of neighbors, the long-haired communards moved north to Island Pond, Vermont, and regrouped. From there the Community has grown steadily and seeded other communes around the globe, including nine in New England alone. Yet neither relocation nor amoebic growth has quieted the controversy. Out of step with the competitive, individualistic strains of contemporary American life, Community members spark suspicion among outsiders wherever they go, and they are often labeled with the term "cult" and accused of a host of sins, from "extreme authoritarianism" to racism, sexism, mind control, child labor and child abuse. When the Twelve Tribes arrived in to Plymouth in 1999, these allegations arrived with it, nipping at its heels, and even a public forum to address community concerns failed to silence the critics—the meeting was interrupted by reports that windows were being broken out of a building members had recently purchased. It took six years of planning and negotiation to open Blue Blinds, and slowly since then, the community has begun to accept the Community and its delicious baked goods.

Sweet apple pie may have played only a small role in this transition to mainstream acceptance, but apples have been an accompaniment for generations of New England religious life. It is hard even to imagine America without them, but when European settlers first arrived, that is just what they found: a landscape that was hauntingly apple free. This absence could not stand. Barely five years after the Puritans arrived, the first English settler in Boston, William Blaxton, reportedly laid out an orchard on Beacon Hill, and when the Boston Bay Company got serious about settling there six years later, it signaled its intentions by ordering a quantity of apples from England to plant, along with other familiar foods such as peaches, plums, filberts, cherries, pears and quince.

Fortunately for the future, this was one instance where New England's rocky soil and forbidding climate turned out to be an asset. While other English crops struggled here, apples thrived, and New England soon welled over in an exuberance of fruit. All across the region, new varieties sprang up with magically local names like Roxbury Russet, Rhode Island Greening, Westfield Seek-No-Further, Hubbardston Nonesuch, Black Oxford, the Nodhead, Rolfe, Sheepsnose and the Blue Pearmain, Henry David Thoreau's favorite. With so many distinct roles in the cuisine, apples became a fully customized fruit, bred selectively to suit each specific purpose. Cidering, snacking, saucing, storage and cooking all demanded different properties, and orchardists selected varieties based on the balance of tartness or sweetness, texture, ripening time, size and color. In the days before industrial agriculture homogenized our crops, there were as many varieties in the applehood as there were orchards, and many were so intensely local as to be virtually unknown outside their community of origin.

The saying goes that the fruit does not fall far from the tree, but in the case of apples, falling near or far makes surprisingly little difference. The seeds may be packed closely together at the core of the apple, but

"Bay Road Fruit Farm (Woman and Apple Tree in Blossom)." *Photo by Frank A. Waugh, circa 1925. Frank A. Waugh Papers (FS 088), Special Collections, UMass Amherst Libraries.*

even adjacent seeds can be radically different genetically, meaning that the trees that spring from these seeds can produce fruit entirely unlike their parents—or one another. Growers looking to produce predictable, desirable fruit forgo seeds altogether in favor of snipping scions from a favored tree and grafting them onto whatever hardy rootstock is available. When those shoots mature, regardless of their roots, they produce fruit just like the tree from which they came.

For Americans, religion has been like these seeds. New sects, new beliefs and entire new theologies have been planted from the seeds of previous sects, only to spring up in wildly variant ways. Today, some Americans find comfort in the claim that ours is a Christian country, but it is a claim that misses the heart of our religious history. Not only does it miss a deep strain of skepticism, anti-clericalism and anti-theism that is too often ignored, but more to the point, it also uses a term, "Christian," that obscures the diversity within. In many cases, the mainstream denominations and evangelical upstarts that dominate traditional accounts of American religious history would exclude many of these new sects from being considered Christian at all, even if those sects consider themselves Christian. What are we to make of the Mormons, Millerites, Spiritualists, Theosophists and advocates of New Thought, all of whom emerged from a Christian stock into something more or less new? Some fit more or less comfortably within the Christian fold; others never have.

Recently, the historian Catherine Albanese has suggested that to understand American religious history, we must look beyond denominations and evangelicals to an equally important third strand in American culture. "Metaphysical religion," she suggested, is as chaotic, diverse and innovative as American apples, and just as influential. According to Albanese, metaphysical religions are typically built around a faith in the powers of the mind and in the mystical interconnectedness of this world and the next, and in some cases, they entail beliefs considered arcane or occult. Examples abound, echoing even in out-of-the-way towns like Whately, Massachusetts, where in 1820 a man described leaving his body and hovering in the sky above to witness his neighbors' sins played out in spirit. "I was a great Angel," he began, "that had two eyes that could see a thousand miles apart." Deeply obscure, this one brief passage from one remote town signals that Americans everywhere found the need to transcend the Christianity with which they were raised to enter the realm of the metaphysical. Sitting outside his body (and sect), the author saw more than he ever could from within. For him, like for many antebellum Americans, sects seemed to exclude as much as include: in reciting their core beliefs, sectarians defined not only who was with them but also who was not. Whether in Whately or Plymouth, metaphysical moments like these have been points of departure for Americans to explore who was truly American.

And yes, apples played a role in this sorting, perhaps most famously in the story of Johnny Appleseed. A staple of fourth-grade readers and Disney cartoons, Johnny Appleseed is familiar and tame—a carefree pacifist dressed in a grain sack with a tin pot on his head, a disheveled vegetarian who gadded about the frontier planting apples wherever he went for the good of future settlers. It is all so fanciful, this myth of one settler's benevolence to those who would follow, this myth of preparing the land for future pies. But Johnny Appleseed was no myth. He was a real sixth-generation New Englander. Born in Leominster, Massachusetts, in 1774, John Chapman was driven by a combination of exigency and opportunity to move ever westward in life, first to western Massachusetts after his father's Revolutionary War service ended and then through New York and western Pennsylvania into the Northwest Territory of present-day Ohio and Indiana, planting apples—whole orchards of apples—wherever he went.

Just why he planted has been a puzzle for historians ever since. For children, the shambolical eccentricity of sack shirts and tin pots are good enough for comic diversion, but since the 1950s, historians have searched for more material motivations. Biographers from Howard Means onward have argued that Chapman's orchards were a way of claiming ownership over lands in the newly opened "frontier," demonstrating that he was improving the land, not merely squatting on it or passing through. Means and later biographers depict Chapman as a shrewd though not always successful entrepreneur who sold or traded trees from his nineteen nurseries for profit. The biographer Robert Price goes further, hinting that the reputation as a crazed though benevolent wanderer may even have been a calculated ploy, a bit of skillful marketing tinged with a hint of Yankee caution. On the frontier, looking penniless was smart, "considering the sums he transported from time to time." For other writers, less materially oriented, Chapman has been imagined as an evangelist who stood outside the bustle of commerce and earthly needs to become, as William Kerrigan wrote, a "propagator not just of apple trees but of northern middle-class reformer values, specifically, piety, usefulness, benevolence, and frugality." There are good points to all of these interpretations.

But Johnny Appleseed was neither simply an apple-obsessed businessman nor a mainstream gospel-spreader any more than members of the Twelve Tribes are simple bakers. There is a metaphysical side to his story that is too easily lost in balance sheets and middle-class concerns. The itinerant apple-peddling of this "New England kind of saint," to use the writer Vachel Lindsay's words, was living his faith in Swedenborgianism, one of the many metaphysical sects that flourished in antebellum America. According to the founder of that religion, the Swedish mystic Emmanuel Swedenborg, we are all part of a universe in which a divine order radiates downward from the spiritual worlds above to our material lives beneath, and divine love washes hourly over all humankind. Descending from higher heavens to lower, each world is an increasingly imperfect version of the one above, but the worlds remain powerfully yoked by a series of "correspondences," connections that are "more than mere symbols" but rather real and dynamic evidence of the ongoing actions of divine love on humanity. Everything that happens in this world, according to Swedenborg, is an echo of a spiritual counterpart above—every fact and feature of worldly life is mirrored in the corresponding spirit above.

Chapman, the Swedenborgian (or New Church) evangelist, was not simply acting the part of a beggar or masking his moneymaking; he saw himself as part of a world of spiritual growth connected to a divine hierarchy of angels above. Sowing apples here, and sowing the Swedenborgian texts that went with them, was nothing less than a counterpart of sowing divine wisdom, laying a divine future for settlers to come. A report on Chapman from a Swedenborgian publication of 1817 made it clear:

He procures what books he can of the New Church; travels into remote settlements, and lends them wherever he can find readers, and sometimes divides a book into two or three parts for more extensive distribution and usefulness. This man for years past has been in the employment of bringing into cultivation, in numberless places in the wilderness, small patches (two or three acres) of ground, and then sowing apple seeds and rearing nurseries. These become valuable as the settlements approximate, and the profits of the whole are intended for the purpose of enabling him to print all the writings of Emanuel Swedenborg, and distribute them through the western settlements of the United States.

When we impoverish our history by writing of America as a Christian nation, we miss the essential stories of John Chapman, Whately and the Twelve Tribes—and many more like them—that have contributed so much to the formation of our country. The wholesome apple, backbone of our cuisine, flooded from New England to all parts of the nation thanks to the metaphysical labors of John Chapman, bringing spiritual light with them. To eat them was to belong, even though we could not all agree just precisely what we belonged to.

Apples may have been harvested in the fall, but through clever breeding for a long shelf life, careful storage or drying, they became available nearly year-round and were a favorite at any time. In her meticulous account of her life between 1785 and 1812, the famous Maine diarist and midwife Martha Ballard recorded making dozens of pies throughout the year—apple, pumpkin and mince appearing promiscuously in winter, summer, spring and fall. They were part of our being. From early on, the popularity of the apple ensured that commercial bakers turned out apple pies in droves, suited to local tastes or whatever the market would bear.

In 1845, the cookbook writer Esther Howland recommended apple pie for Saturday night supper—served with boiled salt codfish as the entrée—and it was listed, too, as a leftover, for the noon meal on Sunday. The pie adapted well to the diversity of New England tastes, whether made with sweet apples or tart, offered cold for breakfast or served with a drizzle of maple syrup, a

Bakery in Manchester, New Hampshire. *Photo by Edwin Locke, September 1937. Farm Security Administration—Office of War Information Photograph Collection, Library of Congress, Prints and Photographs Division.*

dollop of ice cream or a slice of sharp cheese. It has been an essential part of the meal from the earliest days of our republic. Amelia Simmons, the first American to publish a cookbook in the United States, advised that the apple "ought to be more universally cultivated, excepting in the most compactest cities." Every family, she wrote, could fill a "useless" spot in the yard to plant a tree "on which 12 or 14 kinds of fruit trees might easily be engrafted," and the fruit would redound to the benefit of all. "What a saving to the union," she wrote. "The net saving would in time extinguish the public debt, and enrich our cookery."

Not that everyone was enrapt with apple pie. Many writers in the health-conscious antebellum years believed that the fruit was good but the pie bad. The ever-tasteful Sarah Josepha Hale wrote in 1839 that she despised the very notion of turning fruit into pie, although she admitted that apples might be "the only fruit that seems intended for cooking." Stone fruits, never. "And yet women *will make* pies," she wrote, "and mothers *will give* them to their young children, when a bowl of bread and milk, with a little ripe fruit in it, would satisfy their unvitiated appetites better, and in every respect do them much more good…. It is a pity to make these ripe fruits into pies; they would be so much healthier eaten with bread than pie-crust; still they are harmless compared with *meat pies, which should never be made.*"

Nearly fifty years later, Mrs. Lincoln bemoaned the state of apple pie, preferring her fruit straight and unvarnished, even though she recognized the place of pie in our culture. "A simple course of fruit is all that is needed after a dinner," she wrote, "and is much more wholesome than pies. But it is so hard for some people to break away from old customs that it will be long before housekeepers generally will be content to serve the queen of all fruits, the apple, in its natural state instead of making it into the 'persistent pie,' over the preparation of which many women toil, for naught save the fear that they may be considered shiftless if they haven't a pie in the house."

And it was here, in Plymouth, that the old customs seem to have worked so powerfully. After nearly twenty years in town, the Twelve Tribes has settled in and is planning on expanding its operation, receiving town approval for a new two-story café, another store, a private theater and a connecting courtyard. Although it is tax exempt as a religious organization, it voluntarily pays $40,000 annually. It is a persistent pie.

RECIPES

Apple Pie (Child, 1830)

When you make apple pies, stew your apples very little indeed; just strike them through, to make them tender. Some people do not stew them at all; but cut them up in very thin slices, and lay them in the crust. Pies made in this way may retain more of the spirit of the apple; but I do not think the seasoning mixes in as well. Put in sugar to your taste; it is impossible to make a precise rule; because apples vary so much in acidity. A very little salt, and a small piece of butter in each pie makes them richer. Cloves and cinnamon, are both suitable spice. Lemon-brandy and rose-water are both excellent. A wine glass full of each is sufficient for three or four pies. If your apples lack spirit, grate in a whole lemon.

Pie, Apple, with Muscadel Raisins (Lee, 1832)

Peel twenty renneting apples, cut them in quarters, and then cut each quarter into five or six pieces; toss them in a pan with four ounces of sugar in powder, (over which should be grated the peel of a lemon), four ounces of butter lukewarm, and four ounces of fine muscadel plums. Line the edge of a deep dish with a good puff paste, then put in your fruit, and cover your dish with a good puff paste a quarter of an inch in thickness, glaze with the white of an egg, and strew sugar over it. Let it bake an hour in a moderate oven, and serve it hot.

Poor Man's Pie (Aunt Mary's New England Cook Book, 1881)

Butter a pie plate; fill it with sliced apple, and put a crust over it. Bake it, and when done turn it over on to another plate. Sprinkle on the apple a little sugar and nutmeg, and serve hot.

Apple Cream Pie-Crust (A.A. Cook Book, 1895)

Line plate with crust; fill with sliced apples, add ⅔ cup sugar, and pour over it 1 cup cream; grate over it a little nutmeg. Bake without top crust.

Dried Apple Pie (Stonington Cookbook, 1911)

Soak 1 lb. of dried apples over night, boil and mask through a collander. Add 1 lemon, 1 orange chopped fine, a little molasses, and sugar. Nutmeg and cinnamon to taste. Bake in one crust. This makes two pies.—Mrs. E.W. Doty

NOVEMBER

THE PEPO PRINCIPLE

Mothers today, many of them, do not make pies. They aren't particularly interested in pies. Their time is taken up with other things—movies, bridge parties, automobile rides.
—"'Home-Cooking' Made This Man Famous," 1926

Woman is no longer a cook—she has become a can opener.
—"Frederick," 1927

November is the apotheosis of pie, the peak season for pumpkin, mince and apple. The brindle wedge that arrives on the plate, silky and dolloped, perhaps with a stiff peak of whipped cream, needs little introduction. It was as familiar to New Englanders as the pointed firs of our northern woods or our rocky coasts. It is part of our landscape. However far away New Englanders traveled, however long they were gone, they recalled this slice as part of the family. Even in the fruit-luscious lands of the Sandwich Isles, New Englanders clung to their homebound tastes, as Jennifer Fish Kashay argued, turning away from the fresh abundance of pineapple and taro, which they saw as signs of cultural inferiority. Sarah Joiner Lyman, wife of a New England missionary in 1830s Hawaii, rejoiced at receiving the "greatest treat…that I have had since I left the land of my birth, is a pumpkin pie." For Thanksgivings "in Yankee land," according to Sarah Josepha Hale, "the pumpkin pie occupied the most distinguished niche."

This plain and honest pie was not an American invention but rather an adaptation of an old British favorite that goes back at least to the mid-seventeenth century. Complex and somewhat forbidding, these early pies were attuned to the early modern taste for outlandish conflagrations of ingredients, and they satisfied English families for generations. A recipe from the *Compleat Cook* of 1658, for example, was still relevant enough eighty years later to be lifted nearly verbatim by *The Whole Duty of a Woman*, begging the question of whether it was the whole duty to plagiarize. Mixed into the "pompion" custard were "as much Sugar as you think fit"; an assortment of herbs such as thyme, rosemary, marjoram and parsley; and spices that included cinnamon, nutmeg, cloves and pepper. It had a top crust, too, that may or may not have been intended for consumption but that held in the custard as well as layers of thin-sliced apples, currants, butter galore and a caudle of egg yolks and white wine.

In American hands, this overwrought pie was liberated of all hints of French decadence and British opulence. As the wonderful literary historian Rafia Zafar has argued, there was a strong tradition in colonial New England of embracing simplicity in food as a sign of one's spiritual commitments to a simpler, Protestant way of life, and simplicity carried forward into the early national period as a sign of righteous republican restraint versus the excesses of aristocratic Europe. Simplicity in what we wore, what we drank, what we ate and how we wrote were signs that we were zealous converts to cause of the new republic. Pumpkin, this humble fruit that grew readily and heavily in the New World, was our perfect representative and a sure sign of how far we had come from our European roots. Its growing attachment to Thanksgiving cemented it firmly to our image of region and nation.

Even years later, American chefs like James Sanderson (1849) extolled the "immense superiority of the Yankee method" of making pumpkin pie, as well as our willingness to toss off the upper crust and expel the offending apples and other fripperies to enable this "very delicious vegetable" to shine on its own.

No doubt this was the philosophy of Amelia Simmons, author of *American Cookery* (1798). Her ever-so-slight cookbook, "calculated for the improvement of the rising generation of *Females* in America," contained not one but two distinct recipes for pumpkin pie, both stripped to bare essentials. The first was a saturated thing, drenched in a rich custard made of refined sugar, nine eggs and three whole pints of cream, while the second seems aimed at a leaner crowd, using molasses (the less-refined sweetener) to perk up a mere trio of eggs and a quart of plain old milk. Both recipes called for ginger with a hint of variety sneaking through in the secondary spices—the first used mace and nutmeg and the second allspice. This was a pattern for American pies to follow: a stripped-down, pumpkiny custard could either be pumped up into a rich treat or rendered down into an austere hush where the delicate

Right: Pumpkin pies and Thanksgiving dinner at the home of Mr. Timothy Levy Crouch, a Rogerine Quaker living in Ledyard, Connecticut, November 1940. *Farm Security Administration—Office of War Information Photograph Collection, Library of Congress, Prints and Photographs Division.*

Below: Trade card depicting pie delivery on the holiday, circa 1890. *Collection of the author.*

Thanksgiving postcard, with all the nostalgia a person could call for, circa 1920. *Collection of the author.*

fruit shone front and center. Beneath such simplicity and professed unity, however, dissension ran amok. Cooks could agree on spices and could agree to disagree on how rich a pie should be, but there was a long-running feud over whether the starring fruit should be pumpkin or squash.

Pumpkins and squash are distinct species within a large and highly diverse genus, *Cucurbita*, and the spectrum of tastes and textures among them can be enormous. At a good farmer's stand in a New England autumn, it is not hard to see the remarkable variety that has been encouraged among squashes, not just between so-called summer and winter varieties but within them as well. Winter squashes alone range from dark-green acorns and buff bananas to yellow butternut, stringy spaghetti and enamel-hard turbans. The pumpkin species (*C. pepo*) has equally vast variation, as farmers have selected varieties to suit particular markets in color, size, shape and texture.

Looking around that same farmers' market, it may seem as if pumpkin pie has all but eradicated the last vestiges of squash, but there was a moment when squash seemed primed to sweep the New England table. It could have been a contender. Cookbooks from the nineteenth and early twentieth centuries are littered with evidence of squash admiration, and many cooks avowed a strong preference for the humbler fruit over the gaudier orb. Almost any variety of winter squash would suffice, so long as its flesh had a low moisture content and firm texture. A daughter of Roxbury, Massachusetts, and a cooking school impresario in New York, Juliet Corson was among several writers who singled out the green, football-shaped Hubbard squash as particularly prized for pies, although the *White House Cookbook* considered the Hubbard to be no less exalted than the Boston Marrow, an orange-hued squash with buttery flavor and custard texture. Tacitly or explicitly, many insisted that squash was superior to pumpkin without further elaboration.

The bitter contest between squash and pumpkin pie was waged on two additional fronts, even as some cooks sat on the sidelines. To be honest, a few cooks were unsure there was any difference between the two, regarding either as nothing more than a bland medium for the delivery of sugar and spice. There have always been cooks, too, who insisted that the flavor of the fruit could be altered by preparation—which was already arduous thanks to the need to strain the flesh after cooking to ensure that the result was silky, not stringy or grainy. It could be steamed or boiled, no doubt, but many argued that it should be roasted to enhance its flavor.

It was the debate that Simmons foreshadowed, however, about how rich the pie should be that became the focus of long-running skirmishes, and there was plenty of hot sniping over whether cream was called for or just milk, as well as how many eggs made a proper custard. Some cooks admitted to eking by with just a single egg for an unusually skeletal squash pie, while Lydia Maria Child, who had dedicated herself to instructing American women in the virtues of thrift, felt that a frugal three would suffice per quart of milk. Even she, thrifty Lydia, could be seduced by the squash into licentiousness. "The more eggs," she admitted, "the better the pie." Sarah Josepha Hale's five eggs raised the ante, but no one—no one at all—could approach Simmons's nine.

No matter how the fruit was prepared or how rich the custard, both fruits were known primarily as character actors playing a bit role to the headlining act of spice. The dominant note in most squash or pumpkin pies comes from a narrow range of familiar spices: ginger, cinnamon, allspice, mace, cloves and nutmeg. Hale left a bit of room for improvisation, stating that one could include rose water to go with the "cinnamon, nutmeg, or whatever spices you like," while the abstemious Child got down to brass tacks for the thriftiest of the thrifty. "Ginger will answer very well alone for spice," she noted, "if you use enough of it."

Among the five crowning spices, cinnamon was nearly ambidextrous, appearing nearly equally in recipes for pumpkin and squash, while allspice and mace were almost interchangeable and cloves or nutmeg could come and go on their own. If there was a difference between squash and pumpkin pie, it was usually found in the ginger, which was far more common in pumpkin. At least according to Hale, pumpkin was more a spicy thing. Instructing her readers how to make a pumpkin pie, she advised them to "make it like squash pie, only season it higher. In the country, where this *real yankee pie* is prepared in perfection, ginger is almost always used with other spices." In contrast, women all over New England agreed that the dulcet tones of squash outsang the basso profundo of pumpkin. In Farmington, Maine, in 1908, the women of the Daughters of the American Revolution kept their squash practically spiceless, while other women made squash with just a kiss of nutmeg and nothing more. Such muted glory, according to Juliet Corson, was exactly what made the squash preferable: it had a "a less strong flavor" than its orange kin. Bland was beautiful. L.M. Goodnow even advised that blander than bland was an option: "If wished plainer and eggs are not at hand add mere squash and rolled cracker."

We can admit here that many cooks felt like Mary Johnson Lincoln or her peers in the Boston Cooking School who felt that there was no noticeable difference the pies, at least in terms of fruit. Lincoln informed her students bluntly that "Pumpkin Pie is made the same as Squash Pie, using pumpkin in place of squash." Such admirable clarity! Cooks who refused to recognize the difference were sometimes led astray into experiments like the carrot pie, which used carrot in place of squash, but everyone has their limits. The Connecticut-born hydropathic physician Russell Trall commented that carrot pies were "not so delicious as pumpkin pies, though some persons are very fond of them." There was no accounting for taste.

This epic struggle may have been decided permanently in favor of the orange orb only in the 1920s, when so many women seemed to aspire to become can openers. The rise of domestic technologies like electric ovens, stoves, blenders, mixers and refrigerators conspired with the beginnings of modern mass-marketing techniques aimed at home consumers and the advent of processed foods to bring about a shift in our basic habits of consumption. The utopia promised by such new technologies (and new corporate methods) foretold a future in which women would be spared the drudgery of housework in order to devote themselves more fully to family and community—or to cultivation of the self. As historian Samantha Barbas has written, magazines like the *Ladies' Home Journal* and *Collier's* spread a vision in the 1920s of housewives who could turn "their thoughts and energies to other channels" and steer clear of the tendency of flappers and the "Modern Woman" to focus on careers, "clothes, clubs, and climate" rather than housework, children, cooking or any other "'home' stuff." Many, to be sure, saw the allure of flapperdom.

"Yes, this is what makes it possible"

© 1926, THE SERVEL CORPORATION, N. Y.

"Yes, this is what makes it possible." Servel Corporation refrigerator advertising brochure featuring flappers, circa 1927. *McIntosh Cookbook Collection, Special Collections, UMass Amherst Libraries.*

Almost like a pendulum, restaurants in the 1920s began to focus increasingly on "homemade" fare as American tastes at home began to reorient toward foods that were processed, premixed, prepackaged, prepared, precooked and prepurposed. Although the promised utopia turned out to be elusive—new technologies tend only to add new patterns of work—Barbas noted astutely that women began to imagine household economy less as an economy of finance and more as an economy of time. Saving time became more important than saving money. Home economists and the technologies they touted, Barbas argued, offered a way to rationalize the kitchen, to make it more hygienic, more economical, more fitted to the

Whitehead Work-Saving Kitchens advertising brochure, circa 1925. *McIntosh Cookbook Collection, Special Collections, UMass Amherst Libraries.*

family's needs, and many American women threw themselves gladly into the labor- and time-saving gewgaws dangled in front of them, including the premixed ingredients and canned goods that we now know so well.

By plan or happenstance, this became the edge that pumpkins exploited to displace squashy brethren from their "most distinguished niche" at the American table. The signs can be seen as early as 1912, when a fifth column sprang up: dates. Like many food corporations, past and present, the Dromedary Date Company, promoted its product by issuing cookbooks replete with clever recipes for dates used in every conceivable manner (and some inconceivable). In the middle of the *Dromedary Cook Book* was a recipe that loudly announced its loyalty to the all-American holiday, "Thanksgiving Squash Pie." It featured, you guessed it, dates. It is a subtle suggestion, but with squash pie, it is an audacious suggestion. For a dish so pared down over the years to the pure essence of fruit and spice, the presence of an interloper like a date is jarring. Or canning.

Or cunning, for that is what happened next to the squash. While dates were running a rear-guard action, pumpkin made its big move by joining the processing revolution. Canned pumpkin became one of the signal convenience foods of the 1920s, promising a certain consistency of product, with no more stringy pumpkin and no more bits of rind in the mix and certainly no more need for roasting or straining to get the texture right. Introduced by Libby's in 1929, the pumpkin that is most often canned today is a variety specially suited to pie-making, the Dickinson, which is smaller, meatier and thicker-skinned than the average orange globe in our fictive farmers' market. The jack-o'-lanterns carved so hideously on Halloween would yield a wet and stringy mess if cooked and would make for a far from distinguished flavor, but the Dickinson excels for its fine, firm texture.

Canned pumpkin could not have overthrown the squash alone. It needed a collaborator, and it found one in evaporated milk. Although invented before the turn of the century, a relative pioneer in processed foods, evaporated milk only became widely commercially available in the 1920s. In a bold strategic move, evaporated milk joined forces with Libby's canned pumpkin to make the perfect combination for the ultimate convenience food. Equally bold, Libby's followed Dromedary's tactic of offering free recipes to customers to promote its product, pasting a pumpkin pie recipe on its label that has become the de facto recipe for American homes in the past half century. Roped into going pumpkin by the convenience in preparation, Libby's may actually have transformed American taste. Richer than cream and far richer than milk, evaporated milk pairs impeccably with the Dickinson flesh, and ever since, the thinner and more delicate squash has fallen away. Libby's has been so successful with its canned pumpkin filling that commercial farming for this New England fruit has shifted dramatically westward: according to the company, nearly 90 percent of pumpkins grown in this country are grown within an eighty miles radius of its corporate headquarters in Morton, Illinois.

But a secret resistance movement has grown up for all those squash lovers unwilling to surrender, a movement rising from within the complex lineage of *Cucurbita*. Libby's has its own fifth columnist. Although its cans are boldly marked "100% Pure Pumpkin" or "Easy PUMPKIN pie mix," the Dickinson within says otherwise. This Dickinson is no *Cucurbita pepo*; it is actually a variety of *Cucurbita moschata*, a squash by any other name. There is hope yet that the true blandness of New England cuisine will once again prevail.

RECIPES

Pumpkin Pie (Child, 1830)

For common family pumpkin pies, three eggs do very well to a quart of milk. Stew your pumpkin, and strain it through a sieve, or colander. Take out the seeds, and pare the pumpkin or squash, before you stew it; but do not scrape the inside; the part nearest the seed is the sweetest part of the squash. Stir in the stewed pumpkin, till it is as thick as you can stir it round rapidly and easily. If you want to make your pie richer, make it thinner, and add another egg. One egg to a quart of milk makes very decent pies. Sweeten it to your taste, with molasses, or sugar; some pumpkins require more sweetening than others. Two tea-spoonfuls of salt; two great spoonfuls of sifted cinnamon; one great spoonful of ginger. Ginger will answer very well alone for spice, if you use enough of it. The outside of a lemon grated in is nice. The more eggs the better the pie; some put an egg to a gill of milk.

Vermont Pumpkin Pie
(The Woman Suffrage Cook Book, Burr, 1890)

Peel and cut your pumpkin into small pieces and put into a kettle with a very little water, cook from six to eight hours, stirring frequently to prevent burning. When done it should be quite dry and of a rich brown color. Rub through a colander. One quart of pumpkin, three pints of rich milk, four eggs, two and a half cupfuls sugar, one tablespoonful ginger. Bake in rather a slow oven until nicely browned.—Mrs. M.L.T. Hidden

Squash Pie (Hale, 1839)

Pare, take out the seeds and stew the squash till very soft and dry. Strain or rub it through a sieve or colander. Mix this with good milk till it is thick as batter; sweeten it with sugar. Allow five eggs to a quart of milk, beat the eggs well, add them to the squash and season with rose water, cinnamon, nutmeg, or whatever spices you like. Line a pie-plate with crust, fill and bake about an hour.

Squash Pie (Pilgrim Daughters of the First Church, Brockton, 1925)

Note the appearance of brand-name goods in this community cookbook.

Four cups of sifted squash, or 1 can of squash, 2½ cups of sugar, 1 large cracker or two small ones filled fine, 1 teaspoon Slade's cinnamon, 1 teaspoon Slade's nutmeg, ½ teaspoon salt, yolks of 3 eggs, 3½ cups of milk. Beat the whites of eggs stiff and stir in last. Makes the pies nice and brown. Makes 3 large pies.—Mrs. Atwood

Squash Pie (Orange Universalist Church Cookbook, 1928)

¾ cup squash
2 tbsp flour
1 tbsp cream
¼ tsp cinnamon
¼ tsp salt
1 pt milk, heated

Use 1 cup milk to make the above ingredients smooth and add the rest to the following mixture: 1 egg, beaten to a froth 1 cup sugar. Put into squash mixture, sprinkle nutmeg on top.—Mrs. Kenneth A. Wood

DECEMBER

Making Mince

I cannot be alone in the terror I felt as a child over the thought of mincemeat pie. Every year around the holidays, the ghastly pastry would appear at the head of the table, a round leer of golden crust foisted on us by an ancient grandmother oblivious to its shuddering impact. We children were too clever to be duped. Year after year, the pie was ushered onto its doily perch, and year after year it remained undented by our teeth. We were resilient, defiant, and yet while we abstained, the pie haunted our sleep with the inevitable question: what sort of meat is this mince?

Historically, we were not alone in our curiosity. Fear of the meat pie is a transatlantic tradition, and suspicion of what might lie beneath an innocent crust is its deepest root. Whenever a person could not observe a pie being made, "know your pieman" became a watchword for simple self-preservation. A wayward bake shop could inflict any amount of mischief, and prudent pie lovers knew well that when a new bakery opened, it was best to scour the alleyways to ensure the safety of neighborhood cats.

Charles Dickens knew. In *The Pickwick Papers*, Dickens introduced a character, Sam Weller, who extolled the virtues of veal pie (or "weal pie," in Weller's accent), at least "when you know the lady as made it, and is quite sure it ain't kittens." No one, not even the pie man himself, could tell veal from a tender tortie. Weller insisted that he met a pie man who kept a herd of cats for the winter season, when hearty meat pies were in and fruit out and when butchers ran up the price of meat. A deft hand could turn calico, the other white meat, into whatever flavor he pleased:

"It's the seasonin' as does it. They're all made o' them noble animals," says he [the pie man], *a-pointin' to a wery nice little tabby kitten, "and I seasons 'em for beefsteak, weal or kidney, 'cording to the demand. And more than that," says he, "I can make a weal a beef-steak, or a beef-steak a kidney, or any one on 'em a mutton, at a minute's notice, just as the market changes, and appetites wary!"*

In blind dates and books, one never really know what lurks under the covers, but as far as pies go, none has more terrifying hidden potential than the mince, a concoction so medieval in character that it actually is medieval. As food historians Keith Stavely and Kathleen Fitzgerald noted, the pairing of meats and sweets was a favorite at the medieval table, with mince differing from other meat pies only in that the ingredients were, well, minced into a nearly unrecognizable state. Although indecipherable to the naked eye, by the time of the European invasion of New England, the pie's characteristics were well defined: a quantity of meat such as beef tongue or veal was chopped fine with a double quantity of suet; mixed with nearly equal quantities each of apples, raisins and currants; and laced with citrus peel and juice (usually lemon, citron or orange). The meat was usually dainty—tongue and veal were favorites, but boiled beef loin was common—but the pie's distinctive flavor was owed to a suite of inevitable spices (mace, cinnamon, nutmeg and clove) and, in most recipes, to the addition of a jolt of liquor such as claret or the sweet fortified white wine known as sack.

Like so many members of its fraternity, this rich seduction of a pie enjoyed a reputation for great durability, promising an enviable shelf life for its perishable ingredients. Like the mythical fruit cake, this indulgent act of pastry arrived for the holidays and seemed like it might never leave. Sarah Josepha Hale, the writer and propagandist for the Thanksgiving holiday, believed that the mixture of tongue, suet and fruit could be "put down in a stone jar and closely covered" and kept "for several weeks," while the author of *Cookery Reformed* (1755) was convinced that mincemeat could be kept "for some months." Nothing could destroy it. But the pie was durable in another way too: despite individual twists in the recipe here and there, eighteenth-century mince pies could easily be mistaken for ones from a century earlier or a century later. The four pounds of shredded veal and nine pounds of beef suet recommended by *The Compleat Housewife* in 1729, with its mixture of fruits, sugar and citrus (candied peel as well as juice), spice (nutmeg, clove and mace), sack and claret differed only slightly from Hale's recipe from an ocean away and a century later (1838), wobbling only slightly in the proportions of ingredients and in the substitution of good New England cider for sack.

By the time the Pilgrims established Plymouth Colony, this fat-laden, everlasting treat was already firmly yoked in the popular imagination to celebrations, festive occasions and, especially, Christmas. Whenever family and friends gathered for the holidays and the demands of celebration edged out the Spartan day-to-day, mince pies appeared. Britons prized them so highly that they baked them in specially shaped pans, specially suited for their special dish. The author of *The Whole Duty of a Woman* (1737) illustrated more than a dozen such pans in a book otherwise filled with advice for the three stages of a woman's life (virginity, marriage and widowhood)—pans whose "shapes and forms" resemble nothing less than Rorschach blots in three dimensions, ostentatious shapes that would decorate the sideboard and signify a nightmare. Rich and indulgent, this was a festive food, presented with flair.

Being yoked to Christmas and flashy display was hardly a recommendation for the holiday-hating Puritans, who derided mince pies as "idolatrie in crust," according to the historian Janet Clarkson, and tried to ban them. Their qualms, however, did little to dampen ardor for the indestructible mince. Although the Puritans refused to celebrate the pagan holiday, mince survived by shifting its allegiance to Thanksgiving. However much the clergy decried it, the English favorite infiltrated the colonies, and New Englanders went blithely on their sweet-meat way, celebrating and festivating with mince en masse. Here, as in England, the mince pie assumed a coveted spot at the holiday table and become a cultural touchstone for memories of family, friends and home. Mince pie was seldom eaten alone: the earliest American cookbooks feature pies made large enough for small armies or large families. Amelia Simmons (1796) included a mince pie made of calves' feet that weighed in at over eleven pounds, not including the called-for quart of wine, while Mrs. Rundell's 1807 recipe for suet and "scraped beef free from skin and strings"—delicious!—was delivered at more than fifteen pounds.

Everywhere in New England—frugal, austere, Puritan New England—the holidays triggered a Pavlovian response that could be satisfied only by the mass consumption of spiced pies. More than sixty years separated from his native Boston, Ben Franklin could still write to his grandson to say that the approach of Christmas "reminds us of your promise of eating mince Pies with us." For him and his fellow New England ex-pats, the holidays meant mince, and mince meant rich indulgence and family union.

But in New England, too much of a good thing is too much of a good thing. Historically, New Englanders have lauded (if not always lived) frugality, thrift and austerity, and anything that went astray became a potential target for the moralizers among us. To be sure, mince pie continued to have its defenders, like the great reformer Lydia Maria Child, who felt that it could be transformed into an archetype of thrift. In her cookbook *The American Frugal Housewife*, Child insisted that "no economical house-keeper will despise" mince pies since "broken bits of meat and vegetables cannot so well be disposed of in any other way." But in the end, the pie's associations with indulgence were too deep-seated to be dismissed with leftover reasoning. Abigail Adams would have been unimpressed. Writing to her husband, John, in January 1795, Abigail recounted the story of a pious acquaintance, Master Cleverly, who was befuddled when a thanksgiving holiday was declared during Lent, when the pious were expected to fast and renounce luxury. Cleverly "shakes his Head," Abigail wrote, "and says tis a very Arbitrary thing. I suppose he cannot help connecting plumb pudding, Roast Turkey and Minced Pye. He cannot give thanks upon Eggs and fish." Any holiday worthy of the name evoked the siren call of mince pie, and mince pie meant indulgence, even in abstinent Lent. With so many powerful cultural bonds to the sinful dish, anti-pie New Englanders pursued another minced path: if you can't ban the pie, beat the decadence right out of it.

That flint-ribbed New Hampshirite, Sarah Josepha Hale, was one authority uneasy with the mince. Yes, she included it among the recipes in her book, *The Good Housekeeper*, but she did so only from a sense of loyalty to her New England heritage. "The custom of eating mince pies at Christmas, like that of plum puddings," she wrote, "was too firmly rooted for the 'Pilgrim fathers' to abolish; so it would be vain for me to attempt it." She was powerless to resist:

> *At Thanksgiving too, they are considered indispensable; but I may be allowed to hope that during the remainder of the year, this rich, expensive, and exceedingly unhealthy diet will be used very sparingly by all who wish to enjoy sound sleep or pleasant dreams. The dyspeptic should always avoid them as he would his bane, and for children they should be forbidden food; so tempting is the taste, that the only security consists in not tasting. So the "good housekeeper" will be careful not to place the temptation too often before her family.*

One bite and you're hooked. Like many at the time, Hale considered the mince a gateway pie, and although it was indispensable for the holidays, she argued that the caring cook should seek less damaging alternatives.

Fairy Pie, Dougherty's New England Mince Meat novelty advertising brochure, circa 1895.

Fortunately, *The Whole Duty of a Woman* (1737) had already paved the way in dealing with the scourge of indulgence. Among the three recipes offered in the book was a lean mince designed for Lent in which boiled eggs were exchanged for meat. For many writers, as for Mr. Cleverly, the "eggs and fish" were lean, spiritually approved sleights of hand for decadent meat. Lest it was unclear that meat was the spiritual problem, Hannah Glasse's Lenten mince pie performed the swap of eggs for meat, even while leaving the fat, the brandy and sack intact. Apparently, not all pleasures need be renounced.

While some writers wrestled with the spiritual implications of excessive pie, others concerned themselves with health. Even certifiably cat-free mince

Fairy Pie, Dougherty's New England Mince Meat novelty advertising brochure, interior, circa 1895.

pie was dubious—in fact, all pie was. The great Scottish physician William Cullen theorized that humans were physiologically incapable of digesting the heavy crusts of the era, and in the third edition of the *Encyclopedia Britannica* (1797), he was cited as arguing that "very hard and indigestible" pastry was "apt to produce heart-burn and acescency." Just why this was so was a topic for further research, but perhaps, he argued, the physiological reaction was "increased by the burned butter, from a certain sensibility of the stomach, which occasions all empyreumatic oils to be long retained, and so turn

127

rancescent and acid." Add in an overly meaty, over-fatty, overstimulating filling and a dietary disaster loomed.

So it was that meatless mince was born. Fear of spiritual indulgence and fear of health conspired to purge the flesh. Once again Hannah Glasse was a harbinger. Instructing readers how to make mince pies "the best way" in 1767, she relegated discussion of meat to the tail end of the recipe, then specifying that it was only for those who "chuse meat in your pies." Meat was optional in mincemeat. Her culinary competitors were even more explicit. When Elizabeth Raffald issued a new edition of her *Experienced English Housekeeper* in 1778, "mince without meat" made a quiet appearance, and Americans soon echoed: Maria Rundell went meatless in 1807 (and offered a lemon mince to boot, without the alcohol), and eleven years later, Priscilla Homespun offered a "rich mince pie without meat" that sought to keep the façade of rich indulgence behind the lean.

For the full meatless experience, however, it is important to look to the dietary reformers of the Jacksonian era and particularly to the abstemious William A. Alcott, who could wring the joy right out of enjoyment. The thirty years of turbulence that led up to the Civil War saw the first true flowering of vegetarianism in the United States, and Alcott was among its earliest advocates. A second cousin of the Transcendentalist Bronson Alcott (father of Louisa May Alcott) and a close intellectual companion, Alcott was a writer and educator who believed, like his cousin, that adherence to a simple set of rules could spark a wave of "perfect living." In an imperfect age steeped in the desire for creating a perfect society—often attempted, seldom achieved— in an adventurous age of experimentation in controlling the disruptive forces of the body through the practice of celibacy (or free love), Alcott immersed himself in the physiology of consumption. For women and the men in their lives, controlling diet was a key, he reasoned, a key to keeping seething passions in check and mastering the unmasterable will. Just as Alcott hoped one day to see the liberation of the enslaved and the abolition of slavery, so, too, he hoped to experience a liberation from lust through the judicious regulation of intake. Modern cookery, he argued, was simply too rich for the human body to process and too seductive for the human soul:

> It has come to this, at length, that you can scarcely sit down with plain people to what is called a plain meal, and find anything simple. Meat must have been salted and saltpetred, and perhaps smoked; and then it must be cooked with eggs; or if fresh meat or fish be used, it must be tortured into some unnatural shape or other, and peppered and gravied. A pudding of Indian, sweet already

and rich as it ought to be, must have molasses and suet in it; and be buttered and sugared or sauced *afterward. All sorts of pastry must be filled with lard or butter and eggs, and eaten hot, and with butter. Mince pies must consist of eighteen or twenty different articles. Even plain bread cannot be eaten plain. It must be hot, or toasted, or made into pap; and plain fruits, rich from the Creator's hand, must be cooked, or in other words, tortured.*

In Alcott's "rational cookery," simplicity moved us nearer perfection. Obsessed with physiologists' obsessions with overstimulation and indigestion, he proposed that the ideal meal would be a simple affair containing no animal flesh at all, no condiments and little spice, and everything was prepared with as little cooking or combining of ingredients as possible. The "perfection" of diet, he wrote, "consists in having but one article of food, and in having it prepared and eaten in the most simple manner." Like many physiologists, he argued that stimulants like coffee and tea were out, hot food was out, "mixed" dishes of more than one main ingredient were out, alcohol was out, cool water at the table was out and indulgences like chocolate were just too horrid to entertain.

All pie was suspect, but mince pie, oh mince, stood out even among the lowest "substances which…ought never to enter a human stomach." They were beyond redemption, a perpetual imperfection. Once rational New Englanders became awakened to their impact, they would understand that a vegetarian future was the only rational option and would trigger the future perfect:

All meat will become doubtful, and will be abandoned—and perhaps cheese; and milk and all other liquid foods will be used sparingly. Mixed dishes will begin at length to be proscribed. Sausages are already abandoned; but mince pies, hash, seed cakes, plum puddings, plum cakes, and all shortened pie crust, and semi-solid or watery substances, soon follow in their train! And as the taste becomes simplified, the desire for drink, before supposed to be natural, now gradually disappears. The tumbler of water begins to stand untouched till we have done eating, before it is drank off.

Just because humans could eat meat, Alcott argued, there was no excuse for them to do so. "Perhaps, after all, the use of apples chopped fine and mixed with meat, as in mince pies, is as objectionable as any," he wrote. "These mince pies, when made in the best manner, are bad enough; but when made up not only with lean meat, but with the addition of suet, spices, raw and dried fruits, wine, brandy, &c., and put into the usual forms of pastry, they become—as Dr. Paris says of pastry alone—an abomination."

Yet even Alcott recognized that mince pie was wholesome as a symbol, as a reminder of hearth and holiday, and as a sop to mince lovers, he grudgingly offered a "Temperance mince pie" for those not yet ready for true perfection:

> *Its principal excellency consists in the fact, that while it retains all the sensible properties of ordinary mince pie, it is comparatively simple, and contains not a particle of meat or suet, or a drop of wine or spirits; and the crust is of unbolted wheat meal, with no more butter than is just necessary to prevent its adhering to the platter. It is quite a discovery; and is a most happy substitute for the old fashioned mince pie.*

Even this seemed too much for Alcott, who added that mincemeat "is an article which I do not mean to *recommend* to my readers. There are many other better modes of using apples than to use them in any such compound, however great may be its comparative innocency." Although he refrained from invoking cats, Alcott remarked snidely that "very fashionable mince pies" could be found in France, where they were made "from the diseased livers of geese, or other animals. These pies are now brought, in some instances, to this country, especially to Philadelphia, and our other large cities." Here is where the mince hit the road. The connection between "fashionable" foreigners, their diseased pies and our "large cities" is not coincidental. The import of perfidious European ideas had long been feared as a threat to our native republican simplicity and to the purity of the American way of life, and such decadence promised to derail the perfection of our national project. Our swelling, teeming, sinful centers of urban chaos represented the constant change that made antebellum life so challenging and spoke of the loosening of our traditional bonds. Surrendering to the temptations of the city, to its rich allures and complex mixtures of experience were mince incarnate—one could never tell what was under the crust or where it would lead. Worse still, in cities, Americans surrendered *themselves* to the lure of pleasure. Alcott knew where it led:

> *Where is the person, indeed, who does not, by indulging the demands of a pampered appetite, contribute daily and hourly to rivet the chains of her slavery?*
> *And the worst of all is—I repeat the sentiment—woman neither knows nor feels her degradation. Nay, she often glories in it. This is, in fact, the worst feature of slavery; it obliterates the very relish of liberty, and makes the slave embrace her chains. Especially is this so with the slavery of our lusts, and passions, and propensities, and appetites…. She should be infinitely prouder of eliciting a good and enlarged, and noble thought, and a warm, and benevolent, and pious*

sentiment, than of making a mince pie with eighteen different ingredients in it, or of setting a table with forty-five various compound dishes upon it.

In the century after Alcott wrote, meatful mince gradually gave way to meatless, and by the Second World War, tongue and veal had grown increasingly rare. Even as the fearful foods disappeared, terror of the pie lingered, passing through the generation of my grandmother's, the last raised with lustful fats and dainty meats, into the generation of we moderns, naïfs, who are left only with holiday memories and spiced fruit. A meatless mirror of a meaty indulgence seems an unlikely companion, but under the crust, who could really tell?

Recipes

Mince Pie (The Whole Duty of a Woman, 1737)

Take the best Part of a Neat's Tongue parboiled, peel it, cut it in Slices, and set it to cool: To a Pound of Tongue put two Pounds of Beef Sewet and Marrow, then chop 'em all together on a Block very fine; to each Pound of Meat put a Pound of Currants, and a Pound of ston'd raisins, chopp'd or cut small; then pound your Spice, which must be Cloves, Mace and Nutmeg; season it as you like, with sugar, Orange, Lemon and Citron peel, shred with two or three Pippins; squeeze in the Juice of one Lemon, a large Glass of sack, with some Dates, ston'd and shred small; all these being mixed together very well, make your Pies and bake them, but not too much. [A second recipe includes a little verjuice and rose water and, for a third, eggs instead of tongue.]

Mince Pies: A Foot Pie (Simmons, 1796)

Scald neets feet, and clean well (grass fed are best) put them into a large vessel of cold water, which change daily during a week, then boil the feet till tender, and take away the bones, when cold, chop fine, to every four pound minced meat, add one pound of beef suet, and four pound apple raw, and a little salt, chop all together very fine, add one quart of wine, two pound of stoned raisins, one ounce of cinnamon, one ounce mace, and sweeten to your taste; make use of paste No. 3—bake three quarters of an hour.

Weeks after, when you have occasion to use them, carefully raise the top crust, and with a round edg'd spoon, collect the meat into a bason, which warm with additional wine and spices to the taste of your circle, while the crust is also warm'd like a hoe cake, put carefully together and serve up, by this means you can have hot pies through the winter, and enrich'd singly to your company.

Lemon Mince Pie (Rundell, 1807)

Squeeze a large lemon, boil the outside till tender enough to beat to a mash, add to it three large apples chopped, and four ounces of suet, half a pound of currants, four ounces of sugar; put the juice of the lemon, and candied fruit, as for other pies. Make a short crust, and fill the pattypans as usual.

Temperance Mince Pies (Alcott, 1846)

Take one quart of good rye or wheat bread, after it is chopped fine, and one quart of sour apples, chopped fine; add the juice of six lemons, two large spoonfuls of ground cinnamon, a large tea spoonful of salt, a pint of cream or milk, a pint of the best sugar-bakers' molasses, and a pint of washed raisins. Grate in a lemon peel. Bake them one hour.

Mince Meat Pie (Social Union Cook Book, 1900)

Two quarts chopped beef, five quarts chopped apples, two quarts water in which the meat has been boiled, two quarts molasses, two quarts sugar, two quarts cider or sweet pickle syrup, one tablespoon salt, ten teaspoons cinnamon, eight teaspoons cloves, one teaspoon pepper, one teaspoon ginger, one pound suet, two pounds raisins. Chop meat and suet together, add molasses and sugar and cook slowly for two hours or until quite thick, adding apple etc. afterwards. Makes two gallons.—Mrs. E. Merriman

BIBLIOGRAPHY

"Agricola." *The New-York Gardener, or Twelve Letters from a Father to His Son*. Albany, NY: D. Steele & Son, 1824.

———. "Rheum Palmatum, or Pie-Plant." *New England Farmer* 7 (1828): 11.

Alcott, William A. *The Young House-Keeper; or, Thoughts on Food and Cookery*. Boston: Waite, Pierce & Company, 1846

Alden, A., and A. Adams. *The A.A. Cook Book*. 2nd ed. Springfield, MA: Atwood Print, 1895.

Allen, Ann H. *The Orphan's Friend and Housekeeper's Assistant*. Boston: Dutton and Wentworth's, 1845.

"Amenia." "Country Comforts." *New York Times*, July 9, 1853, 3.

American Gardeners Magazine 1. "On the Cultivation of Rhubarb (*Rheum Raponticum*)" (1835): 247–49.

American Restaurant Magazine. "'Home-Cooking' Made This Man Famous" (1926): 80.

Ames, D.F. "Pie-Plant, or Rhubarb." *New England Farmer* 13 (1834): 2.

Anderson, Peter. *An Inaugural Dissertation on the Diarrhoea Infantum*. New York: Tiebout and O'Brien, 1795.

Appadurai, Arjun. "How to Make a National Cuisine: Cookbooks in Contemporary India." *Comparative Studies in Society and History* 30 (1988): 3–24.

Aunt Mary's New England Cook Book. Boston: Lockwood, Brooks & Company, 1881.

B., B. "Strawberry-Rhubarb Pie." *Boston Globe*, June 11, 1914, 13.

B., J. "Pie-Plant." *New England Farmer* 9 (1831): 220.

Barbas, Samantha. "Just Like Home: 'Home Cooking' and the Domestication of the American Restaurant." *Journal of Food and Culture* 2, no. 4 (2002): 43–52.

Barton, Benjamin Smith. *Elements of Botany*. Philadelphia, PA: printed for the author, 1803.

Bayley, Richard. *An Account of the Epidemic Fever which Prevailed in the City of New York, During Part of the Summer and Fall of 1795.* New York: T. and J. Swords, 1796.

Beecher, Catherine E. *Miss Beecher's Domestic Receipt Book.* New York: Harper, 1850.

————. *A Treatise on Domestic Economy, for the Use of Young Ladies, at Home, and at School.* Rev. ed. New York: Harper, 1848.

Bliss, Mrs. *Practical Cook Book.* Philadelphia, PA: Lippincott, Grambo, 1850.

Bradley, Alice. *Electric Refrigerator Menus and Recipes.* Cleveland, OH: General Electric Company, 1927.

Brown, Henry Collins. *Valentines Manual of the City of New York.* Vol. 3. New York: Chauncey Holt Company, 1919.

Brown, Nellie I. *Recipes from Old Hundred; 200 Years of New England Cooking.* New York: M. Barrows and Company, 1939.

Burr, Hattie A. *The Woman Suffrage Cook Book.* Boston: Hattie A. Burr, 1890.

Cambridge Cook Book. Cambridge, MA, [1909?].

Campbell, Tunis G. *Hotel Keepers, Head Waiters, and Housekeepers' Guide.* Boston: Coolidge and Wiley, 1848.

Canning, Josiah Dean. *Thanksgiving Eve.* Greenfield, MA: Merriam and Mirick, 1847.

Carrol-Parsal Wheel of the Second Congregational Church. *The Wheel Cook Book.* Oak Park, IL: Second Congregational Church, 1913.

Carter, Charles. *The Compleat City and Country Cook: or, Accomplish'd Housewife.* London: A. Bettesworth and C. Hitch, 1732.

Carter, Susannah. *The Frugal Housewife.* Philadelphia, PA: James Carey. 1796.

Chesbrough, Mary Mott. *The Chicago Record Cook Book.* Chicago: Chicago Record, 1896.

Child, Lydia Maria. *The American Frugal Housewife.* Boston: Carter and Hendee, 1830.

Clarkson, Janet. *Pie: A Global History.* London: Reaktion Books, 2009.

Collingwood, Francis. *The Universal Cook: City and Country Housekeeper.* London: R. Noble for J. Scatcherd and J. Whitaker, 1792.

Colonial Daughters Chapter No. Seventeen, D.A.R., Farmington, Me., D.A.R. Cook Book. Farmington, ME: Knowleton & McLeary, 1908.

The Compleat Cook Expertly Prescribing the Most Ready Wayes, Whether Italian, Spanish or French, for Dressing of Flesh and Fish, Ordering of Sauces or Making of Pastry. London: E.B. for Nath. Brook, 1658.

Confederate Receipt Book. Richmond, VA: West and Johnson, 1863.

Congregational Church (Phillips, Maine). *Social Union Cook Book.* Phillips, ME, 1900.

Cornelius, Mary Hooker. *The Young Housekeeper's Friend.* Boston: C. Tappan, 1846.

Corson, Juliet. *Miss Corson's Practical American Cookery and Household Management.* New York: Dodd and Mead, 1886.

Crockett, Walter Hill. *How Vermont Maple Sugar Is Made.* St. Albans, VT: Department of Agriculture of the State of Vermont, 1915.

Crowen, T.J. *Every Lady's Book: An Instructor in the Art of Making.* New York: J.K. Wellman, 1946.

Dromedary Cook Book. New York: Hills Brothers Company, 1912.

Duffield, Mary B. *The Home Messenger Book of Tested Recipes.* Detroit: E.B. Smith & Company, 1878.

Elliott, Charles. *A Trip to Canada and the Far North-West*. London: W. Kent and Company, 1887.

Emerson, Lucy. *The New-England Cookery, or the Art of Dressing All Kinds of Flesh, Fish, and Vegetables*. Montpelier, VT: Josiah Parks, 1808.

Estes, Rufus. *Good Things to Eat*. Chicago: self-published, 1911.

Farmer, Fannie. *The Boston Cooking-School Cookbook*. Boston: Little, Brown and Company, 1896.

———. *Food and Cookery for the Sick and Convalescent*. Boston: Little, Brown and Company, 1904.

Flagg, Wilson. *A Year Among the Trees, or, The Woods and By-Ways of New England*. Boston: Estes and Lauriat, 1881.

Frederick, Christine. "'Vamping' Hubby from His Home." *Cafeteria Management* (December 1927): 11.

Frigidaire Recipes, Prepared Especially for Frigidaire Automatic Refrigerators Equipped with the Frigidaire Cold Control. Dayton, OH: Frigidaire Corporation, 1928.

Gardiner, Abbe. *Mrs. Gardiner's Receipts from 1763*. Hallowell, ME: White & Home, 1938.

Gaylord, Willis. *American Husbandry*. New York: Harpers, 1841.

Glasse, Hannah. *The Art of Cookery*. London: W. Strahan, J. and F. Rivington, J. Hinton, 1774. First published in 1747.

Goodnow, L.M. *The Housekeeper's Assistant*. Cambridge, MA: John Ford & Son, 1873.

Greenbaum, Florence Kreisler. *The International Jewish Cook Book*. New York: Bloch Pub. Company, 1919.

Gvion, Liora. "What's Cooking in America? Cookbooks Narrate Ethnicity, 1850–1990." *Food, Culture and Society* 12 (2009): 53+.

Hale, Sarah Josepha. *The Good Housekeeper, or The Way to Live Well and to Be Well While We Live*. Boston: Weeks, Jordan & Company, 1839.

———. *Ladies New Book of Cookery*. New York: H. Long & Brother, 1852.

Harris, Florence L. *Pies a-Plenty*. Garden City, NY: Blue Ribbon Books 1949.

Hibbard, Laura B., and Mary Alice Vaughan. *Home Cookery, Representing the Experience of the Women of the Congregational Church*. Laconia, NH: Laconia Press Association, 1904.

Hill, Benson E. *The Epicure's Almanac; or, Diary of Good Living…*. London: How and Parsons, 1841.

Homespun, Priscilla. *The Universal Receipt Book*. 2nd ed. Philadelphia, PA: Isaac Riley, 1818.

Howes, Ethel Puffer. *The Dinner Kitchen Cook Book*. Northampton, MA: Smith College, 1930.

Howland, Esther Allen. *The New England Economical Housekeeper, and Family Receipt Book*. Cincinnati, OH: H.W. Derby, 1845.

Johnson, Mary. *Madam Johnson's Present: or, Every Young Woman's Companion in Useful and Universal Knowledge*. 4th ed. Dublin: printed for J. Williams, 1770.

Kashay, Jennifer Fish. "Missionaries and Foodways in Early 19th-Century Hawai'i." *Food and Foodways* 17, no. 3 (2009): 159–80.

Kirmess Cook Book. Boston: Women's Educational and Industrial Union, 1887.

Kitchiner, William. *The Cook's Oracle; and Housekeeper's Manual*. New York: J. & J. Harper, 1830.

Knott, Charles C. *Sketches in Prison Camps: A Continuation of Sketches of the War*. New York: A.D.F. Randolph, 1865.

Ladies Aid Society of the Baptist Church (Wallingford, Vermont). *Choice Selection of Tested Recipes from Many Households*. Morrisville, VT: Wm. H. Nichols, 1907.

Ladies Aid Society of the Norwich, Massachusetts Baptist Church. *Book of Tested Recipes*. Norwood, MA: self-published, 1907.

Ladies of Resolute Grange and Vicinity, Brownville, Maine. *Resolute Grange Cook Book*. Brownville, ME: Resolute Grange, 1913.

Ladies of St. Mary's Guild of Grace Church (Providence, Rhode Island). *Choice Receipts*. New Haven, CT: Geo. D. Bone & Son, printer, 1905.

Ladies of the Congregational Church (Newport, Vermont). *New Memphremagog Cook Book*. Newport, VT: Ladies of the Congregational Church, 1907.

Ladies of the Congregational Church (Rutland, Vermont). *Excelsior Cook Book*. Rutland, VT: Tuttle, 1891.

Ladies of the First Baptist Church (Gloucester, Massachusetts). *Reliable Receipts for the Housewife*. 3rd ed. Gloucester, MA: Printed at the Cape Ann Breeze Office, 1900.

Ladies of the First Congregational Society (Keene, New Hampshire). *The Keene Cook Book (No. 2)*. Keene, NH: Sentinel Printing, 1898.

Ladies of the Second Congregational Church (Biddeford, Maine). *Three Hundred and Fifty Tried and Tested Formulas*. Biddeford, ME: Time Steam Job Print, 1886.

Ladies of the Unitarian Church (Waterville, Maine). *Collection of Delectable Recipes, Tried and True*. Waterville, ME: Waterville Mail Office, 1898.

Land, Leslie. "Boston Cream Pie." *Yankee Magazine* (1983).

Lee, N.K.M. *The Cook's Own Book*. Boston, Munroe and Francis, 1832.

Leslie, Eliza. *Miss Leslie's Complete Cookery*. 38th ed. Philadelphia, PA: H.C. Baird, 1851.

———. *Seventy-five Receipts for Pastry, Cakes, and Sweetmeats*. 3rd ed. Boston: Munroe and Francis, 1830.

Lincoln, Mary Johnson Bailey. *Mrs. Lincoln's Boston Cook Book: What to Do and What Not to Do in Cooking*. Boston: Roberts Brothers, 1883.

Loughead, Flora Haines. *Quick Cooking*. New York: Putnam, 1891.

Madden, Etta M., and Martha L. Finch, eds. *Eating in Eden: Food and American Utopias*. Lincoln: University of Nebraska, 2006.

McCulloch-Williams, Martha. *Dishes and Beverages of the Old South*. New York: McBride, Nast & Company, 1917.

McWilliams, James E. *A Revolution in Eating*. New York: Columbia University, 2007.

Mendenhall, P.H. *The New Bedford Practical Receipt Book*. New Bedford: C. Taber & Company, 1859.

M'Mahon, Bernard. *American Gardeners Calendar*. Philadelphia, PA: Graves, 1806.

Moore, Helen Watkeys. *Camouflage Cookery: A Book of Mock Dishes*. New York: Duffield and Company, 1918.

New York (City) Mayor's Committee on Food Supply. *How to Use Leftovers*. New York, 1915.

New York Times. "In a Den of Rattlesnakes." August 16, 1880, 5.

———. "William Thompson Dead: He Accumulated a Fortune as a Manufacturer of Pies." June 8, 1903, 7.

Parloa, Maria. *Appledore Cook Book.* New ed. Boston: A.F. Graves, 1880.

———. *Miss Parloa's Kitchen Companion.* 19th ed. Boston: Estes and Lauriat, 1887.

———. *Miss Parloa's New Cookbook: A Guide to Marketing and Cooking.* New York: C.T. Dillingham, 1882.

Petrin, Ronald A. *French Canadians in Massachusetts Politics, 1885–1915.* Philadelphia, PA: Balch Institute Press, 1990.

Phillips, Henry. *History of Cultivated Vegetables.* London: H. Colburn, 1822.

Putnam, E. *Mrs. Putnam's Receipt Book: And Young Housekeeper's Assistant.* New York: Phinney, Blakeman & Mason, 1860.

Raffald, Elizabeth. *The Experienced English Housekeeper.* London: R. Baldwin, 1778.

Reliable Flour Company. *Reliable Recipes No. 2.* Boston: self-published, 1907.

Ruiz, Andrea. "Table Talk Pies: A Favorite for Over 80 Years." Suite. https://suite.io/andrea-ruiz/5aed2gs.

Rundell, Maria Eliza Ketelby. *American Domestic Cookery.* New York: E. Duyckinck, 1823.

———. *A New System of Domestic Cookery, Formed Upon Principles of Economy, and Adapted to the Use of Private Families.* Boston: W. Andrews, 1807.

Rush, Benjamin. *Medical Inquiries and Observations.* Philadelphia, PA: Thomas Dobson, 1796.

Salmon, William. *The Family Dictionary, or, Household Companion.* 4th ed. London: H. Rhodes, 1710.

Sanderson, James M. *The Complete Cook.* Philadelphia, PA: Lippincott, 1849.

Sayers, Edward. *The American Fruit Garden Companion.* Boston: Weeks, Jordan and Company, 1839.

Simmons, Amelia. *American Cookery.* Hartford, CT: Simeon Butler, 1798.

Sisters and Friends of Oak Lawn Grange, No. 42, P. of H. (Oak Lawn, Rhode Island). *Oak Lawn Grange Cook Book.* Providence, RI: T.S. Hammond, 1914.

Smith, E. *The Compleat Housewife, or, Accomplish'd Gentlewoman's Companion.* 3rd ed. London: J. Pemberton, 1729.

St. George, Donna. "Boston's Dowdy Pie Takes the Cake Again." *New York Times,* January 22, 1997, C1.

Staveley, Keith, and Kathleen Fitzgerald. *America's Founding Food: The Story of New England Cooking.* Chapel Hill: University of North Carolina, 2004.

———. *Northern Hospitality: Cooking by the Book in New England.* Amherst: University of Massachusetts, 2011.

Stoneham Grange, No. 326, Patrons of Husbandry. *Cook Book.* Stoneham, MA: George R. Barnstead, 1919.

The Stranger's New Guide through Boston and Vicinity. Boston: Charles Thacher, 1865.

Strasser, Susan. *Never Done: A History of American Housework.* New York: Pantheon, 1982.

Theosophical Society, Los Angeles Lodge. *Vegetarian Cook Book.* 2nd ed. Hollywood, CA: Theosophical Publishing House, 1919.

Thoreau, Henry David. *Wild Apples and Other Natural History Essays.* Athens: University of Georgia, 2002.

———. *Winter.* Boston: Houghton Mifflin, 1891.

Trall, Russell T. *The New Hydropathic Cook Book.* New York: Fowler and Wells, 1854.

Tried and True Cook Book. 2nd ed. Andover, MA: Andover Press, 1913.

Trollope, Frances. *Domestic Manners of the Americans.* London: Whittaker, Treacher and Company, 1832.

Vegetarian Cookbook. Benton Harbor, MI: City of David, Israelite House of David, 1956.

Volunteer Women of the Navy Relief Society, San Diego Auxiliary. *Favorite Recipes of the Navy and Marine Corps, San Diego Area, Including a Collection of Representative Mexican and Old San Diego Dishes Contributed by Descendants of Early Settlers of San Diego County.* San Diego, CA: The Auxiliary, 1950.

Warner, Anne. "Pies in General and a Few in Particular." *Good Housekeeping* 37 (1903): 590–91.

Warren, Jane. *The Economical Cook Book: Practical Cookery Book.…* New York: Hurst, 1881.

Wayside Gleanings: A Handful of Wheat, Collected for the Benefit of the Junior Auxiliary to the W.B.M., Mass. 2nd ed. Orange, MA: C.A.J. Waterman, 1889.

Whitney, Daniel H. *The Family Physician, and Guide to Health.* Penn Yan, NY: H. Gilbert, 1833.

The Whole Duty of a Woman, or, An Infallible Guide to the Fair Sex. London: T. Reed, 1737.

Young People's Society of Christian Endeavor. *The Stonington Cookbook.* Stonington, CT: Second Congregational Church, 1911.

Zafar, Rafia. "The Proof of the Pudding: Of Haggis, Hasty Pudding and Transatlantic Influence." *Early American Literature* 31 (1996): 133–49.

INDEX

ABOUT THE AUTHOR

A recovering paleontologist, onetime molecular biologist, wayward poet and sometime historian and archivist, Rob Cox has worked as head of special collections at UMass–Amherst. In a checkered career before arriving in Amherst in 2004, Cox held positions at the University of Michigan (where he received his PhD in history) and the American Philosophical Society, acquiring strong interests along the way in the histories of religion and science. He has written on topics ranging from talking to the dead in the nineteenth century to the plants of the Lewis and Clark expedition and Quaker relations with the Seneca nation in the 1790s. His most recent work includes a trilogy of books on New England culinary history and, quite separately, the history of sleep.